On Texas Backroads

= = = = = = = =

STORIES FOUND ALONG THE WAY

CARLTON STOWERS

Cover photograph ©2016 Doug Hodel Photography

ISBN: 978-0-9973706-2-1

Printed in the U.S.A.

Published by TexasStarTrading.com
174 Cypress St., Abilene, Texas 79601
info.texasstar@yahoo.com
(325) 672-9696

For Pat, whose fingerprints are on every word,
and Adam Pitluk and Glenn Dromgoole,
friendly chance-takers...

The majority of these pieces first appeared in *American Way*, the in-flight magazine of American Airlines. Here and there are musings that were published in the *New York Times, Dallas Morning News, Houston Chronicle, Abilene Reporter-News* and a dandy little magazine called *Texas Co-op Power.*

In an attempt to retain the flavor of the time and mindset in which each essay was written, I've stubbornly resisted the urge to do vigorous tinkering. When a need cried out, however, I've attached a brief postscript to a few of the tales.

Carlton Stowers

Contents

= = = = = = = =

Foreword

= = = = = = = =

In this simply-but-beautifully written collection of essays about people and places in his native Southwest, Carlton Stowers provides a page-turning treat for the reader. A 21st Century literary Marco Polo, he travels the highways and byways, stopping at the site of what the old-timers claim was an honest-to-goodness UFO crash in Aurora, Texas, a ghost town (Thurber, Texas, Pop. 4), recalls a book burning in Sweetwater, visits pet cemeteries, Mary's Café in Strawn where finger-licking chicken fried steak is served, a game called six-man football...

Well, you get it. He has a genuine interest in an incredible range of subjects – the origin of Fritos, raccoons roaming in the attic of his house, the first Conrad Hilton hotel (a small red brick building with cracker-box rooms in Cisco, Texas), grandmothers and the important role they play in today's society, Pelham, Texas, one of the last all-African American communities, walks in the neighborhood on a cool late afternoon with the scent of new-mown grass in the air and friendly dogs greeting their "pal" with tail-wagging happiness.

The famous, the well-known?   Sure. The author tells of

meeting with his childhood hero, Roy Rogers, and wife Dale to help write their autobiography, *Happy Trails*. And how about that reclusive author, Robert E. Howard, who lived with his parents in Cross Plains, Texas, and escaped his loneliness by creating the fantastic Conan the Barbarian? Or an Olympic gold medalist-turned-Hollywood stuntman?

Carnegie libraries? The glory days of pinball machines? The Terlingua World Chili Cook-Off Championship down in the Big Bend? There is something here for everyone.

So sit back and enjoy the ride along Stowers' incredibly entertaining backroads.

— Elroy Bode

Heartland

= = = = = = = =

FEBRUARY 2012

Time was when they were scattered throughout the emancipated South, tiny enclaves far removed from the urban byways, little more than dot-on-the-map reminders of a historical transformation that was often overlooked by a nation busily congratulating itself for having set free its slave laborers. These small all-black settlements, hidden down backroads, were the gateway to freedom.

Pelham, Texas, just over an hour's drive south of glitzy and ever-growing Dallas, was one of those communities that sprang to life back in 1866 after landowners allotted each of their slave families 200 acres of rich cotton and grain farmland on which to begin new lives. And with that, they built a community. In time, there were a couple of churches, a general store, a grocery, cotton gin, cafe and community center. As the population steadily grew to an estimated 325 residents they recognized the need for education, prompting the hiring of teachers and building of a small two-story frame structure that housed the elementary students downstairs and the senior school students upstairs.

By the early 1900s, Pelham thrived. Crops were bountiful, new businesses opened, there was regular mail delivery and telephone service. Residents worked hard and played hard. The Pelham High Panthers basketball team soon gained a reputation that spread far beyond the flatlands of the little town it represented. In the summers, the local baseball team played in its own ballpark and produced such standouts as shortstop Elmer McMullen, who later was a semi-pro star in California in the days before the major leagues welcomed black athletes into the fold.

And unlike so many of the nation's all-black communities that faded to memory in the 1960s once a more enlightened nation adhered to the concept of integration in its schools and workplaces, Pelham remains. Today it is one of the nation's last all-African American communities. Not because of lingering anger over long ago social injustices or any aversion to mingling with other races, but because for the 35-40 who still call it home it remains their heartland.

Alfred Martin, the town's self-appointed historian, understands better than most. The grandson of a slave who could neither read nor write, he was born in Pelham and, except for a time when he sought higher education in a San Antonio junior college and briefly the University of Minnesota and serving as a member of the flight line crew for the legendary Tuskegee Airmen in Alabama during World War II, it has been his home.

And he has been an eyewitness to its changing.

Pelham today is far different from that of his childhood, little more than a faint reminder of times past. The thriving businesses are gone. Across Farm Road 744, the Pelham School is now a museum, filled with photographs, genealogy archives and artifacts of a time gone by. The sound of children laughing long ago fell silent.

Asked the mean age of those who still residing in Pelham, Martin smiles as he mentally pictures his neighbors, a finger pointing in the direction of each house that remains. "Let's see," he says, "82...93...85...80..." Only the elderly, now past days of tending fields and watching the town grow, remain.

He was, he says, the last in the community to retire after once farming as many as 2,000 acres. Today his and the sprawling fields owned by friends are leased out to a new generation of farmers who reside in nearby towns like Corsicana and Hubbard. There is a degree of irony and a signal of social progress attached to the fact that those now tilling the soil and harvesting the crops are white.

There is, in truth, no longer need for the isolation of a Pelham, no cause to shrink from the outside world that has become a rich melting pot of races. "It's a different world altogether for black people," Martin quickly volunteers. "Now, there's opportunity everywhere one looks."

And that, he says, pleases him greatly. Still, one must have a comforting place to call home. For Alfred Martin and the declining number of his neighbors, Pelham, Texas, established 146 years ago, still serves that need. And will likely continue to do so until all are gone and it, too, quietly vanishes into a historical footnote.

* * *

(Since this piece was originally published, the population was reduced after three of Martin's Pelham neighbors died. Now 92, his hearing isn't what it used to be, but he still enjoys recalling the history of his birthplace.)

The Perfect Day
= = = = = = = =
AUGUST 2009

It was one of those short-sleeve days when the sky was blue and cloudless, spring finally making its arrival on a warm, gentle breeze; a week-ending day too ideal, too seductive to squander indoors. Just a short drive away, on the tiny and picturesque campus of Northwood University, a doubleheader was scheduled.

I phoned my grandson, freed from the classroom by some magic called "teacher's in-service day," and suggested we go watch a little baseball. An eight-year-old sports fanatic, he eagerly accepted my invitation and said he would be waiting in his driveway, shooting baskets.

Northwood, hidden away on the outskirts of the Dallas suburb of Cedar Hill, is one of those under-the-radar universities where 1,116 undergraduates quietly work toward business degrees in a bucolic setting. The 43-year-old campus is bordered by carved-out hillsides and shaded by ancient trees that, were it not for the array of modern buildings and student housing, would make it look more like a nature center than an academic outpost. Its baseball team, the Knights, compete in the Red River Athletic Conference, a NAIA (National Association of Intercollegiate Athletics) league that is on the bottom rung of the college sports pecking order.

While the baseball field is beautifully manicured, there are no lights for night games. Its wooden bleachers might accommodate 100-150 fans, and to those who come, admission is free. It is rare when even their scores are printed in the *Dallas Morning News*. Here, they play the game for the sheer joy of competition and the welcome respite it offers from academic pursuits.

As young Price and I sat among 20-or-so other spectators (a few girlfriends, a parent or two, a handful of faculty members and one retiree with a friendly Chocolate Lab on a leash), I was delighted by my grandson's unabashed enthusiasm. He cheered the home team, pored over the single page program listing the names and positions of the players, marveled at a towering home run that cleared the centerfield fence *("Man, Papa, he smashed that one, didn't he?)*, chased down a couple of foul balls, and assured me that the chili dog from the student-operated concession stand was the best he'd ever had.

Following the first game, the Knights coach and several of his players quickly set up a portable table behind the home dugout and soon sandwich makings and fruit were spread for the athletes' between-games snack. One of the Northwood players, noticing my admiring grandson, walked over to say hello. It was Christmas morning on a springtime afternoon. Price was blissfully wandering in his own Field of Dreams.

As time leisurely passed and thoughts of the outside world

briefly disappeared, I answered a steady stream of questions: *What's their record so far this season? Did the players for the other team ride on the bus that was parked across the way? What's the coach saying to the pitcher? Did you think that was a hit or an error?*

And, most importantly: *When do they play again?* I silently knew we'd found our occasional getaway destination for the steadily warming weeks that lay ahead.

The sun had slid behind a nearby cliff as the second game ended with the Knights scoring a one-run victory over the visiting Oklahoma City University Stars. The teams had split the doubleheader. Lengthy shadows began to spread across the campus as my grandson watched the players walking toward the field house where hot showers and continued celebration awaited. On the way to the car we stopped at the nearby tennis court to briefly watch as a friendly doubles game was winding down. Then I felt a tug at my arm. Price pointed toward the outdoor basketball court located next to a small stream that wound through the campus. "Nobody's playing," he observed. "My basketball's in the car."

It wasn't difficult to pick up on the not-too-subtle hint. We retrieved his ball and were soon engaged in our first game of H-O-R-S-E. It wasn't even close as Youth easily triumphed over Age. Same with the second game. And the third.

Dinnertime, I knew, was fast approaching as the glorious day began to fade to evening gray. The baseball field was now empty, silent. The tennis players were gone. Somewhere across the way, students were settling in to study. It was just us — an eight-year-old boy and an old man, breathing in the sweet smell of the new season, listening to the gentle sounds of the night birds as they began to welcome the fast approaching darkness.

"Your grandmother's cooking chicken and dumplings," I mentioned as we began our departure.

"Can I eat at your house?"

"If your Mom and Dad say it's okay," I replied, "you certainly can."

On the short ride home, Price, tired but clearly content, sat admiring the foul ball he'd retrieved and been told he could keep. "This," he said with that smile that never fails to melt my heart, "was really fun."

A bit more experienced and worldly, I graded it higher: It was perfect.

* * *

(In 2014, Northwood University closed its doors in Cedar Hill, silencing the cheers for the baseball Knights. Today, I spend my spring afternoons watching my grandson play second base for his high school team.)

Patron Saint

= = = = = = = =

AUGUST 2012

Stay at this business of writing and public speaking long enough and the clutter of small prizes and gifts becomes one of life's certainties. Visiting Rotary and Lions Club luncheons, book club gatherings and writers' conferences, one is sure to collect enough coffee mugs to stock an all-night diner, pens galore and Certificates of Appreciation by the box-load. Along the way you can be assured an endless diet of rubber chicken, green beans and grateful handshakes from the guy saddled with the endless responsibility of rounding up the Speaker of the Week.

Occasionally. however, something out of the ordinary occurs.

Not long ago it was my privilege to say a few words at a celebration of local emergency responders, an event filled with waving flags, parading fire engines and ambulances and a cheering crowd of men, women and children there to demonstrate appreciation of those who work to keep us safe. It was not an invitation for which I expected to receive another token of gratitude. At the program's end, however, Cedar Hill, Texas, fire chief John Ballard approached, offered a few kind words for my brief talk, and pressed something into my hand.

Only after I'd returned home, coat and tie discarded, did I take a careful look at the small bronze medallion he'd given me and began to wonder of its origin and significance.

On its front was a relief of a muscular Roman soldier, staff in one hand, pouring a pitcher of water onto a blaze from the other. Printed along its edges were the words "Saint Florian: Patron Saint of Firefighters."

I was curious to learn more.

Visit www cyberspace and you'll learn that, according to the legend, the Austria-born Florian was a noble and brilliant officer in the Roman army, performing heroic deeds, even miracles of healing, as he quickly rose to the rank of general. His downfall was his Christian belief in a time when the orders of the day were to round up all members of the faith and swiftly sacrifice them to the Roman gods. Florian's refusal ultimately resulted in his being flogged and thrown into the Enns River with a rather heavy stone tied around his neck.

In 1138 he was elevated to sainthood by Polish Pope Lucius II. Among the mythology that preceded his after-life fame was the story of how Florian had once managed to douse a raging fire with only that single pitcher of water. Adding to the firefighting mythology would be the story in which a latter-day Polish fireman called out the saint's name as he rushed into a burning building to rescue its occupants. In time, then, Saint Florian would gain worldwide recognition as the patron saint of those who fight fires.

The legend, I can only assume, is true. Whether Saint Florian actually looks down on those who battle fires, large and small, I have no idea. But the fact remains that we all, regardless of religious bent or superstitious need, want to think there is some invisible hand on our shoulder, protecting us from bad times and harm's way. If a talisman kept in a pocket or attached to a chain around one's neck offers some measure of comfort and confidence, I applaud and endorse it. Perhaps we might all be better served to embrace the notion famed author Jim Harrison refers to as the "ecstasy of belief."

Long a talisman of firefighters throughout Europe and the eastern cities in the United States, the Saint Florian medal's popularity has spread greatly in the past decade. In Cedar Hill, says fire marshal Randal Jordan, one is presented to each new training graduate, given to honor all promotions, and for over-and-above deeds performed.

"Everyone in the department has one and carries it," Jordan says. "Some wear the medals around their neck, some carry them in their pockets, others keep them in their equipment bags."

So now, when a late-night silence is broken by the wail of a fire engine racing somewhere to tend whatever new tragedy has invaded the darkness, my thoughts go to my own prized medallion. And I sincerely hope that Saint Florian, wherever he might be, is on the job.

Walking on the Wild Side

= = = = = = = =

MAY 2013

In the cool of the evenings, when the sun has faded to a dull shade of orange and the gentle scent of new-mown grass mixes with the fragrance of crape myrtle and lantana, I walk a familiar route through my neighborhood. A long-standing routine, its purpose is more to clear the mind from the workday and breathe the fresh air than any prescription for good health. I'm not training for anything.

People with dogs on leashes stop to say hello. Familiar barking voices call out from windows and backyards as I pass, as if to warn that I'm invading their territory and all trespassers would be wise to keep moving. They half-heartedly bark the same warning day after day, month after month. It's their job.

It is the animal sights and sounds I most look forward to on my daily trek. My wife chides me about being on a first-name basis with more dogs than neighbors. There's Rusty and Cherokee, Peanut and Rainey, Oreo, Jazzie, Brownie, Maggie and Shadow, to name a few. They come in a variety of breeds, sizes and ages and are always tail-wagging happy to meet a fellow traveler. We're pals.

Then, as I venture beyond the sidewalks and paved streets into the nearby cedar woods, the faces and sounds change. It becomes a musical nature walk, with the occasional evening hoot of an owl, a dove cooing a summons to its mate or the rat-tat-tat sound of a woodpecker still hard at work, the "caws" of a gathering of crows arguing over something. Occasionally, a lonesome coyote, emerging from a creek bed to begin his evening forage, will stop to stare from a careful distance. High above, a pair of red tail hawks, wings spread majestically, will glide through the last flickerings of daylight. And frisky squirrels play a final game of chase along the limb of a favored pecan tree before calling it a day.

And for some reason, viewing this offers reassurance that, regardless of the day's misadventures and doom-saying headlines, my small part of the world somehow remains in balance.

I am comforted by these creatures, both tame and wild, and pleased to co-exist with them. Even the decision by a family of raccoons to temporarily take up lodging in the attic last summer was but a mild irritant. Sitting nightly, watching as the mother and her young peeked from their hiding place and then paraded in lock-step across the rooftop to roam the neighborhood became an anticipated fascination. In time, however, their rustling night sounds made sleep impossible and, feeling no small amount of guilt, I lured them into a trap cage and drove them to a nearby lakeside park, hopeful that the new location would be more welcoming. In short order, I turned my attention to an opossum who daily performed his balancing act along the backyard fence. And when a night-creeping armadillo visited and decided to burrow into a new home beneath the front porch, it was as much amusing as a concern. I finally named him Alfred and decided we could get along.

There is beauty in these animals' simple routines and needs and grace in their ability to adapt to the fact so much of their habitat has been cut down, graded over and built up. I'm fully aware that mankind has invaded their turf with endless housing developments, shopping centers, soccer fields and parking lots, but am no spitting angry environmentalist. I've never hugged a tree and you'll not find a "Save the Earth" bumper sticker on my automobile. I have no agenda, just a genuine appreciation for the quiet pleasures I daily encounter along my way. Truth is, I'm pretty comfortable with the way things are.

I will continue to dutifully fill the squirrel and bird feeders located at strategic spots in the yard and put out food and water for a couple of neighborhood cats who visit but show no interest in becoming friends. I like them much better than they seem to like me.

That's fine, too.

And so, as long as now-aging legs are willing, I shall continue my evening journey, along the same familiar and welcoming path where friends, old and new, await. In doing so I find great peace.

John Wilkes Booth: Gone to Texas?

= = = = = = = =

JUNE 2011

Be forewarned that the following tale does not appear in any of those dry-bone American History textbooks you read back in the day. It's a tad murky on the dates you were required to memorize and usually isn't given so much as a footnote by the tweedy Civil War Era scholars. When asked, they generally grumble and quickly lump it in with the Roswell UFO Crash, Bigfoot and black helicopter sightings.

The general consensus, remember, is that John Wilkes Booth, the celebrated Washington-based thespian, fired the shot that took the life of President Abraham Lincoln on that April evening in 1865. He then jumped from the President's Box – suffering a fractured leg in the process – and fled from the Ford Theater. Twelve days later, we're told, the authorities tracked him to his hiding place in a northern Virginia tobacco barn where he was shot and killed. End of story, case solved.

Not so fast. What about the whispered theory that Booth performed his evil deed at the behest of government conspirators who wished their leader assassinated and, as part of the deal, agreed to help the gunman escape?

To buy into such a notion one has to go to Texas, where tall-tale conspiracy theories and unsolved mysteries are produced like cotton and cattle. As the story goes, that's where a very alive John Wilkes Booth landed in the aftermath of his crime. Old-timers in the lakeside community of Granbury, just south of Fort Worth, have been passing the story along for generations.

It actually begins in the South Texas town of Bandera where, according to journalist Logan Hawkes, a man named John St. Helen arrived and opened a private school where he not only taught students the three R's but classic literature and acting as well. According to the legend, he also fell in love with a local lady and they were to be married – until she mentioned that among the guests she had invited to the wedding was a relative who was a U.S. Marshal. St. Helen fled town in the dead of night.

Later he surfaced in Granbury, where he gave up the academic life and became a saloon keeper. St. Helen, according to researcher Gary Hancock, walked with a noticeable limp, often quoted Shakespeare to patrons of his bar and every April 14 – the anniversary of Lincoln's assassination – got falling down drunk.

He became seriously ill in 1877 and, certain he was dying, confided to a friend, lawyer Finis Bates, that he was not John St. Helen but, rather, John Wilkes Booth. He even told the attorney where he had hidden the gun used to kill the president. According to the folklore, Bates located the gun, finding it wrapped in a newspaper which carried an account of the events at the Ford Theater.

Surprisingly, St. Helen/Booth regained his health and vigorously denied ever making his death bed confession. Then he high-tailed it out of town again, arriving in the Oklahoma community of Enid, where he took a room in a local boarding house. His name, he told the landlady, was David. E. George.

HistoryBuff.com's R.J. Brown writes that for 26 years George called Enid home before again becoming gravely ill. As a January 1903 issue of the local *Enid Wave* reported, a dying George admitted to his landlady, identified in the article only as Mrs. Harper, that he was John Wilkes Booth. When word reached old friend Bates, he quickly traveled to Oklahoma and immediately recognized the deceased as the man he'd long ago known as John St. Helen.

Bates later wrote a book, published in 1908, that put forth the theory that the man who had once confessed to him was, in fact, Booth. It sold well — and developed a divided following of believers and naysayers. Having gained possession of the body, he had it mummified and for several years allowed it to be displayed as a touring carnival sideshow attraction.

Which, most debunkers insist, was where it — and the story that accompanied it — deserved to be.

Michael W. Kauffman, author of *American Brutus*, considered the definitive work on Booth, is among them. "Pathetic and twisted though it is," he says, "Booth did, in a sense, achieve his goal of great notoriety. He's managed to live long beyond the grave."

Pride Restored

= = = = = = = =

NOVEMBER 2011

There is no scientific formula by which we pick our sports heroes. Some of us with high mileage nostalgically cling to the memories of yesteryear stars, men with names like Ben Hogan and Babe Ruth or Jesse Owens. Those with a more contemporary point of view tick off the achievements of modern day giants like Payton Manning or Muhammad Ali or maybe Michael Jordan.

You can have them all, past and present. Me, I'll take a guy named Jeff Harrell.

No, you'll not encounter him on the banquet circuit or see him on ESPN's highlights. He hasn't been asked to endorse a single product. He gets no celestial payday for his accomplishments and, truth is, it took him a long time to arrive at his shining moment.

Harrell, now in his 70s, today a grandfather, is the reigning Senior Games national discus champion in his age group. He's the guy all us washed-up jocks wish we could be, a competitor who finally found a way to rebound from a lifetime of athletic disappointments and near misses.

"All my life," he admits, "I'd wanted to be the best at something."

And, back in the day, he came close. He was 13 when he took the mound for his Brownwood, Texas, All-Star team, needing but one more playoff victory to earn a berth in the 1954 Little League World Series. A week earlier, he'd thrown a no-hitter, striking out 13 Carlsbad, New Mexico, batters. Then, however, his control deserted him and he and his teammates lost, 5-3. The dream visit to Williamsport, Pennsylvania, was cancelled.

As a schoolboy he tried other sports with marginal success but baseball was his passion. By the summer of 1960, the 6-2, 160-pound Teenage League right-hander had a fastball that had scouts promising a bright future as a pro. There were no radar guns to chart his speed in those days, but it was clear he could bring the heat. The summer before he signed with the Philadelphia Phillies for a $25,000 bonus, the 18-year-old Harrell had struck out 156 batters.

The quest for fame and fortune, however, died a slow, agonizing death. In his second trip to the mound in the rookie Pioneer League, on a 33-degree night unfit for baseball, he felt a sudden sharp pain in his right shoulder, a signal that his rotator cuff had been badly torn. This, understand, was back in a less enlightened time when any kind of surgery was considered an immediate ticket out of the game. Goodbye fastball. Goodbye hopes of making it to the Big Leagues.

For the next seven years he bounced around the minors, playing in outposts like Spartanburg, Bakersfield and Chattanooga, but his signature pitch never returned and his career peaked in Class AA.

"I stayed with it as long as I did, not so much because I thought I'd miraculously get better," he recalls, "but because I had no idea what I'd do with my life once I put sports behind me." He was 26 when he retired and moved home to Brownwood to settle into a career as recreational director at a school for wayward youngsters.

The constant ache in his shoulder was his only reminder of his athletic days. Finally, at age 57, he chose to have surgery to repair the damaged rotator cuff.

"A few years later I was watching a track and field meet on television and made an off-hand remark to my wife that I really missed being in some kind of competition." Daneilia told her husband of 48 years about a friend whose husband had begun participating in something called the Senior Games, an age group track and field competition. "That," she said, "might be something fun for you to do."

Unsure that he could get back in shape, he began taking long walks, then lifting weights. Finally, he experimented with throwing the discus. Eventually, he began entering various Senior Games meets.

Over the past decade, he has lost only once. Then, last spring at the National Senior Games, Harrell not only won his event but established a new meet record.

"Competing again has added years to my life," he says. "And being a national champion feels really good. It's restored a little pride."

And made him an inspiration to aging couch potatoes everywhere.

* * *

(After recently undergoing two shoulder surgeries, the now 74-year-old Harrell has returned to training, looking ahead to the 2017 National Senior Games. The national age group record he set in 2011 still stands.)

Flop House to Penthouse

= = = = = = = =

MARCH 2013

Barring a long overdue notification from the Publishers Clearing House Sweepstakes, great fortune is destined to pass me by. Our lot in life is to stand aside, keep the mortgage payments current, and enviously admire history's great entrepreneurs like the Rockefellers, DuPonts, Hearsts and Carnegies. And, of course, legendary hotel empire-builder Conrad Hilton.

It was the latter's remarkable success story that recently drew me to the edge of the small Texas town of Cisco (population 3,709), just a couple of hours west of Dallas, for a look at a red brick building that has stubbornly survived since it was built in 1916. Originally called the Mobley Hotel, the box-like two-story structure's first purpose was to accommodate weary laborers during the region's historic oil boom days.

Hardly an architectural wonder, once called "part flop house, part gold mine," it is where Hilton began his remarkable career.

The old Mobley, with its 41 crackerbox rooms and a small dining area, was the first hotel he owned, launching what would grow into a glitzy international chain.

The dynasty was not so much planned as the result of a fortuitous turn of events.

As the story is told by local historians and Hilton himself in his *Be My Guest* autobiography, the 32-year-old New Mexico native had traveled to Cisco in 1919 with plans to buy the town's bank. When, upon his arrival, the owner upped the previously agreed-upon asking price, Hilton balked, said no thanks and angrily went in search of a night's lodging before catching a train back home.

He couldn't even get in the front door of the nearby hotel. Exhausted oil field workers were renting rooms in eight-hour shifts. Some even slept, heads down on the dining room table, or in the chairs in the small lobby.

Fascinated by what he saw, Hilton sought out proprietor H.L. Mobley and learned he had grown weary of running the hotel and was anxious to seek greater fortune in the oil business. Conrad offered him $40,000 – just over half of what he'd planned to spend on the bank – and suddenly became a hotel-owner. During the next four years, he resided in Cisco, learning the inn-keeping trade and soon began to envision a chain of hotels that would ultimately spread to Dallas, New York, Los Angeles, then internationally. In time, the Hilton name became the gold standard of the industry.

It was, however, not so much the resounding success he would enjoy in his colorful lifetime that fascinated me. Rather, it was the artifact of his beginning.

Today, the 97-year-old Mobley stands proudly at the end

of what is now called Conrad Hilton Avenue, refurbished, spit-polished and serving as a museum, community center and office of the local Chamber of Commerce. It is now listed on the National Register of Historic Buildings.

But not before it suffered through woefully hard times. In the years following the demise of the oil boom and Hilton's leave-taking to bigger and better things, it was sold and re-sold, serving briefly as a boarding house, a retirement home and even the winter residence of an Alaskan gold miner. In time, however, it fell vacant and unwanted, a weed-guarded eyesore. At one point a $5,000 offer was made by a construction worker whose plan was to tear it down and salvage the bricks.

Coming to the rescue was a generous grant from the California-based Hilton Foundation which joined with Cisco's history-minded city fathers to begin rehabilitating the building into a lasting monument to the hotel business legend. With proper small town pomp and circumstance, it re-opened in 1986.

Sitting in his office, where the old hotel's dining room was once located, museum curator John Waggoner dispatches encyclopedic knowledge of Cisco's bygone days. He can recite the history of the old hotel, down to some of the famous people, like humorist Will Rogers, who lodged there. Did you know that band leader Lawrence Welk launched his career in Cisco? Or that in the holiday season of 1927 a man dressed in a Santa Claus suit led a daring robbery of the bank?

And, he says, visitors from throughout the U.S. and 20 foreign countries have stopped in. Among them: Hilton's son Eric, grandsons Conrad III and Steve and, most recently, granddaughter

Linda, who is now director of culture and values for Hilton Worldwide.

And how did they react upon seeing the birthplace of the family patriarch's dream? "After Linda toured the museum," recalls Waggoner, "she sought me out and gave me a big hug." It was enough said.

The Great Hamburger Debate

= = = = = = = =

OCTOBER 2011

Just what investigative organization's jurisdiction the debate falls to is unclear, but it is high time somebody gets on the ball and once and for all sets this culinary issue to rest. The public has the right to know just who gave this country one of its greatest and most time-honored backyard cook-out and fast food chain traditions.

Who, we ask, should be rightfully credited as the originator of the hamburger? Can we please finally solve this twisted mystery and get on with the striking of a medal to show our appreciation?

For decades now we've had several claimants to the honor, each with a sizable and energetic group of Chamber of Commerce and Historical Society backers pleading their respective cases. The citizens of New Haven, Connecticut, for instance, are certain that the first full-meal deal was served at Louis Lassen's café back in 1900. Bah Humbug, say the historians in Seymour, Wisconsin, who claim their very own Charlie Hagreen was selling his burgers to appreciative local customers as early as 1885. Two years earlier, some argue, brothers Frank and Charles Menches were peddling burgers at the Summit County Fair in Akron, Ohio. And in Tulsa, they insist that Oscar Weber Bilby cooked the first hamburgers for neighbors attending a Fourth of July celebration on his farm.

Then, there's Fletcher Davis who called picturesque little Athens, Texas (75 miles southeast of Dallas) home. For my money, he's the leader in the clubhouse. Here's why:

To do proper detective work on the matter, one must first understand the definition of a true, All-American hamburger: Ground beef patty, mustard and/or mayonnaise, tomato, lettuce, pickles and onions served between two slices of a warm bun and generally accompanied by an ample side order of fries and catsup. Simple enough your kid can recite it, right?

History tells us that all but Fletcher Davis simply served up steak sandwiches; a piece of meat slapped between a couple of slices of plain bread. I know I'll get letters, but, folks, a hamburger that ain't.

Davis not only used the above-mentioned recipe, but his achievement is the best documented of the cases. The story goes that so impressed were Athens visitors to his town square cafe that they chipped in to fund his trip to the 1904 World's Fair in St. Louis. There, he set up a stand near the midway and sold his wares. Even a reporter from the *New York Tribune* took note of the gourmet discovery and questioned Davis extensively about his burgers as well as asking for details about the accompanying fries. Not used to being interviewed, Uncle Fletch, as folks back home knew him, explained that he'd borrowed the fried potato recipe from an old friend who lived in Paris. It never occurred to him to differentiate Paris, Texas, from Paris, France. Thus in his article, the reporter, unfamiliar with Texas geography, referred to the side dish he'd sampled as *"French* fried potatoes."

Even the experts at Hamburger University, McDonald's corporate school in Oak Brook, Illinois, embrace Davis as the likely inventor of the burger they now sell the world over. Before knowing Davis by name, its researchers concluded that "a food vendor at the 1904 St. Louis World's Fair was the first to introduce the sandwich to the public." That "vendor," as we know, was none other than Fletcher Davis. And, rest assured, these folks don't take their fact-finding lightly. As McDonald's founder Ray Kroc says, "We take the hamburger business more seriously than anyone else."

And if that's not official enough for you, be aware that in 2006 the Texas Legislature passed a resolution recognizing Davis as the originator of the hamburger. In Athens there's a historical plaque that boasts of the achievement. For years they've celebrated the milestone with Uncle Fletch's Burger Cook-Off during the city's annual Fall Festival. Texas legends like historian Frank Tolbert and millionaire former Dallas Cowboys owner Clint Murchison, Jr., were convinced enough to tell Davis' story in their own writings.

So, barring indisputable evidence to the contrary, Uncle Fletch, former potter-turned-cook, is our man. And, despite what calorie-counters might tell you, the world is ever better for his history-making contribution.

Homage
to Heroes

= = = = = = = = =

SEPTEMBER 2012

Be aware that the following is the result of years of careful research and daily observation that has resulted in a conclusion which, while hardly new, begs a reminder. We are constantly told of the stellar achievements of gifted artists, high finance movers and shakers, political power barons, those who keep us from harm's way and people who can cook up a storm. We are a people who celebrate our heroes and rightfully so.

Some, however, perform their services outside the spotlight's glare.

Thus, our subject today is grandmothers, something about which I know a great deal inasmuch as I've now lived with one for a number of years. Like bestselling author Judith Levy says, they are born the minute a new child comes into the world. And, Lordy, do they play an important role in today's society. They go by a variety of names, including Granny and Grandma. In France they're called Meme, the Germans and Dutch lovingly refer to them as Oma. The one at my house is called Nana, and I am amazed by the range of easy talents she brings to her position. Not to mention the energy.

On any given day she is sitter and taxi service, official family photographer at soccer games, dance recitals and choir performances, the go-to lady when cakes need to be baked for favorite school teachers or a birthday party requires a planner. If the elementary school teacher needs a volunteer, guess who gets the call? She patiently serves as summertime lifeguard at the backyard pool, no matter the soaring temperature, and can sew up a Halloween costume that'll be the talk of the neighborhood.

It is to her table that the grandkids, along with their moms and dads, gather to celebrate Thanksgiving and Christmas dinners. And all the while she somehow manages to avoid the pitfall of crossing the fine line drawn by parents keenly aware of the difference between interfering and helping out.

And she'll be the first to tell you she is but one of many doing the same.

In an economic time when it is increasingly necessary for both parents to work, it is often the grandmother who steps in to pinch hit. According to AARP, in fact, no fewer than 4.5 million American children are being raised solely by grandparents of those whose parents deserted the responsibility of child-rearing for myriad reasons.

"The grandmother's role is constantly evolving," says AARP spokeman Rafael Ayuso. "From being the primary care-giver to those filling in for the parents who are away at their workplace, she's playing an ever-growing part in the child-rearing process.

Her input ranges from simply being friends and playmates to offering needed stability to the children. She's become the family's safety net."

So, we're not talking about the Hallmark-inspired portrait of the lil' ol' lady who does nothing more than spoil the kids rotten with sweet talk and chocolate chip cookies. Today she's a far more complex figure in the family picture. She is teacher and comforter, someone with time to hear childhood concerns about school day activities and imparts wisdom not yet achieved by Mom and Dad. She knows what to do about upset tummies and scraped knees, commands manners and respect, stresses the importance of learning the ABCs, advises against taking shortcuts when a school project is due, and instinctively knows when to cheer or gently scold.

Her knowledge of things is remarkable, ranging from the most simple way to unravel the mysteries of fifth grade math to how to repair broken dolls and get stains out of baseball uniforms. She can immediately recognize the fluid mood of whichever grandchild arrives at the front door, knowing whether to talk or listen, suggest a dip in the pool or get homework done. It's a gift. Grandmothers, it seems, just know those things.

Mine did. So did Nana's. She admits that even today she still occasionally has warm and welcomed dreams about carefree childhood summers spent at her grandmother's house.

You'll pardon the unscientific observation, but perhaps it is simply a divine skill passed along through generations, an instinctive awareness of the importance of the job to be lovingly done. Whatever the case, we're all – my grandkids included – immensely better for it.

Bite-Size History

= = = = = = = = =

NOVEMBER 2010

For the most part, our historians have done a commendable job reminding us of the milestone achievements that have greatly impacted American lives. We know that Thomas Edison brought us out of the darkness with the invention of the light bulb. Were it not for Alexander Graham Bell, our kids couldn't talk endlessly on the phone. We've duly credited Henry Ford for freeway traffic jams and the Wright Brothers for giving us irritating airport congestion and countless flight delays.

But in no history book can I find mention of Charles Elmer Doolin and his Depression Days brainstorm that forever changed our nation's eating habits. You ask me, the guy deserves a statue and a parade.

True, he may not have done my waistline much good, but over the years he's added greatly to my enjoyment of county fairs, ball games, fishing trips, late night TV watching, backyard cookouts and long cross-country drives. His food-on-the-run invention has been my constant companion since boyhood days.

Think about it for a minute: Where would we be today without his crispy, salted corn chip Fritos? If there was a Snack Food Hall of Fame, Doolin would get my vote for immediate induction.

His proud daughter, Kaleta, an accomplished Dallas artist and careful keeper of the family history, agrees. Her dad and his story are, she rightfully boasts, a need-to-know part of Americana. And she's the go-to source for how it all came about; has even written a book, *Fritos Pie: Stories, Recipes and More.*

You want an honest-to-goodness success tale, she's got a dandy.

In the early '30s, C.E. Doolin was proprietor of San Antonio's Highland Park Confectionary, constantly in search of new ways to lure customers into his establishment. In addition to the pastries, ice creams, soft drinks and candies he had to offer, he wanted some kind of bite-sized treat he could place on his counter for arriving patrons.

Down the street, at a neighborhood service station, Gustavo Olguin had just the thing. From Mexico, Olguin had brought the idea of a popular Mexican "beach food" that he cooked, packaged and sold. It wasn't exactly the culinary version of rocket science. He simply cut tortillas into small strips, deep fried and salted them, then put the crispy chips into small bags. Records show that he had a grand total of 19 customers.

Aware that Olguin wanted badly to return to homeland Mexico and his love of coaching soccer, Doolin offered to buy him out. After considerable negotiation, the owner agreed to sell his recipe, customer list and cooking utensils for $100 cash.

Doolin's only problem was getting his hands on that kind of money.

Which is where his mother, Daisy Dean Doolin, enters our story. Demonstrating remarkable faith in her son's plan, she offered to pawn her wedding ring, an above-and-beyond gesture that raised $80. Elmer and his brother, Earl, came up with the additional $20 and thus was born The Fritos Company.

Its first headquarters was Daisy Doolin's kitchen when 10 pounds of Fritos (loose Spanish translation: *fried things*) could be produced daily. Priced to sell for a nickel per package, a good day's profit was two bucks.

That, as we historians like to say, was how it all began.

In the years to come Doolin became consumed with the notion that he had struck a food product gold mine. Eventually, production moved into a rented building that would house Doolin-designed cooking facilities, assembly line conveyor belts, a packaging process and its own test kitchen for continued experimenting with the recipe. He even began growing and testing various types of corn in his search for the perfect masa.

"We kids were his taste-testers," recalls Kaleta. "He'd bring samples home, straight off the conveyor belt."

Fritos were a hit in the Doolin home as well as in food outlets nationwide. Not just as a snack but as an ingredient for recipes Daisy Doolin was coming up with to be printed on the back of each package. There was her Fritos Meatloaf, Fritos Squash and, most important, her famed Frito Pie, that simple and tasty treat that remains the favorite of every high school football stadium concession stand in the nation. You don't even need to write it down to remember it: Open a pack of Fritos, pour in a little chili, stir and enjoy. I can do it with my eyes closed.

But, back to our history lesson.

In 1934, the far-sighted Doolin moved his operation to Dallas and ultimately had a fleet of delivery trucks on the road. By 1950, Fritos were sold in every state in the U.S. A decade later, distribution had expanded to 48 countries.

Such was the ever-growing demand that he eventually sold a dozen manufacturing franchises. Among those who bought in was Herman Lay, a Nashville businessman who was also pioneering in the snack food business. If you bought a bag of potato chips back in those days, it most likely distributed by Lay's company.

Ultimately, it was at Lay's suggestion that the companies merged into what would become the famous and mega-successful Frito-Lay Company.

Not a bad return on a $100 investment.

Friday Night Lite

= = = = = = = = =

AUGUST 2005

As the Friday night lights again shine on that end-of-summer Texas ritual known as high school football, a lion's share of the public attention will focus on the multimillion dollar stadiums, the six-figure-salaried coaches and the 17-year-old superstars carrying the dreams of their winning-is-everything fandom on their shoulders. In a state which loudly boasts that it produces the premier players and teams in the country, it is big-time, high-dollar, pressure-filled and, some critics lament, out of control.

But not completely.

In rural hamlets throughout the state, and across a large swath of the Great Plains, teen-agers compete in a game called six-man football, keeping alive the spirit when schoolboy sports were simply played for fun.

Six-man is limited to tiny towns where enrollment at the local high school is 99 students or less. And the athletic budgets and talent pool are best described as Friday night lite.

Yet in 100-plus public schools in Texas – and others in New Mexico, Colorado, Nebraska, Wyoming, Montana and Saskatchewan – there remains a welcome and reassuring purity accompanying the sport, which was the hybrid invention of a Nebraska high school coach named Stephen Epler. Back in the mid-1930s, Epler saw a need for country boys at schools too small to field a team with the customary 11 players and devised a way it could be played with six.

It is a fast-paced, hard-hitting sport where final scores often resemble those of basketball. The field is 80 yards long, as opposed to the usual 100; all players on offense – three backs and three linemen – are eligible to carry the ball and receive passes; and there is a "mercy rule" to prevent unnecessary embarrassment — if at any point in the second half a team leads by 45 points, the game is called.

No player is turned away because he lacks size, speed or special talent. A 125-pound freshman is likely to line up alongside a 200-pound senior. Rosters rarely rise above a dozen or so players. Russell Hall, coach of the Morgan, Texas, squad, had only the minimum six players on the school bus he drove to one out-of-town game. Some less fortunate schools have had to cancel seasons when injuries and academic shortcomings reduced their roster below the number necessary to field a team.

"There was a time in the mid-'50s," says Granger Huntress, keeper of a web site called sixmanfootball.com, "when there were thousands of small schools in the United States playing the game." Today, because of America's rush to urbanization and the deaths of so many farming communities, the nationwide total has been reduced to roughly 250. But in Texas hamlets like Penelope, Panther Creek, Apple Springs, and Blanket – as well as at a growing number of private schools too small to field a regular team – the sport continues to have its place.

Off winding farm roads, nestled adjacent to cotton fields and pastureland, fans gather in stands built to seat no more than a couple of hundred. Some watch from lawn chairs, sit on sideline blankets or in their pickup trucks, honking approval each time a touchdown is scored. From concession stands, the aroma of Booster Club-grilled burgers wafts through the night air. Small children romp and play behind the end zones, their parents comfortable that they are nearby and safe. And it isn't unusual for referees to briefly halt a game to shoo someone's wayward dog from the playing field.

Jack Pardee, a former NFL linebacker and Washington Redskins coach, was a member of the Christoval, Texas, six-man team in the early 1950s, once scoring nine touchdowns in a game that was played in the town's rodeo arena. "Six-man football is what small town life in Texas is all about," he says. "It provides kids with the wonderful experience of being part of a team and an important part of the community."

Some time ago, in May, Texas, I talked with Robert Cramer, a retired geologist who played his first six-man game as a teenager in Hardy, Nebraska. "In those Depression times," he says, "folks paid a dime to come and watch our games." The price of admission has risen to $3 at some stadiums these days, but that's about the only difference.

"Football was important to our little town," said Raymond

Czirr, a teammate of Cramer's in those days. "Fact is, it was what kept it going."

Three quarters of a century later, many of those who gather to cheer their six-man teams say much the same.

Searching
for Conan
= = = = = = = =
JUNE 2011

In an endless quest for pop cultural enrichment I've attended Willie Nelson's Fourth of July Picnic, a Black-Eyed Pea Festival or two, Rattlesnake Roundups, comic book conventions now and then and more Chili Cook-Offs than a grown man should admit to.

Nothing, however, can compare to an annual June weekend event called Robert E. Howard Days, held in the little West Texas community of Cross Plains. And, before we go any farther, be aware that I wasn't there just to kick up my heels. Nope, this was a trip with purpose. Those of us in the business like to call it Investigative Journalism.

As you're no doubt now aware, yet another movie based on the swashbuckling, dawn of time character Conan the Barbarian will soon arrive at your neighborhood multiplex. This time it stars a heroic and muscular Jason Momoa instead of Arnold

Schwarzenegger (who had played the title role in two previous Conan movies), and marks yet another milestone in a remarkable yet little-known career of a writer named Robert E. Howard.

Never heard of him? No wonder; it's been 75 years since he wrote a word. He died in 1936 at age 30, committing suicide upon learning that his mother was near death. Yet worldwide his legacy is one of the most amazing in the history of the written word.

The reason for the 25th annual gathering of fans, scholars and movie folks from as far away as Sweden, France, Germany and Russia in little Cross Plains (population 1,000) was to honor the man who once lived there with his parents in a little white frame house that still sits on the edge of town. There, Howard biographer Mark Finn tells us, the strange and tragic young man young wrote furiously on an old Underwood typewriter, creating a genre that would eventually be known as sword & sorcery fiction.

He was at his peak in the Depression Days, sometimes writing 12,000 words in a single day, selling his fast-paced, action-filled stories of a mythical land in a prehistoric Hyborian Age to pulp magazines like *Weird Tales* for a penny a word. In addition to Conan, among the 800 short stories he authored were also bigger-than-life characters like Solomon Kane, Kull and Red Sonja. They're all still around today in book form, comics, and on motion picture and television screens.

This guy might never have won a Nobel Prize or Academy Award, but his work has sold a ton of books and a lot of popcorn around the world. Kids read Marvel Comics versions of his stories, scholars pour over every poem, short story and novel he rapidly produced back in the '20s and '30s, and his works are as well read today in Poland, Japan and the Netherlands as they are in the

U.S. If you're a collector and can locate a first edition of his debut novel, *A Gent from Bear Creek*, for sale, be prepared to fork over something in the neighborhood of $5,000.

So, how could someone stranded in a dusty oil and cotton patch town imagine such tales?

Sitting near the restored Howard house, author James Reasoner is among those who continue to marvel at the depth of Howard's imagination. "One of the great fascinations about his work lies in the fact that he had an isolated, rural Texas background yet was able to create this amazing fantasy world," he says. "I've been traveling to Cross Plains since 1995 and have come to realize that a good deal of the geography he describes in his stories can be actually found here in West Texas."

Fellow author Finn agrees. A regular at Howard Days for two decades, he says he made a determined effort in his biography, *Blood & Thunder*, to make readers aware of the influence of Texas on the writer.

Fedrik Malberg, Swedish producer of the latest Conan movie, says, "The themes of Robert E. Howard are as relevant today as they were when he wrote them back in the '30s: one man picking up his sword to do justice and right wrongs. It's an everlasting theme."

For fellow Texan Finn, it is one of the things of which he is often reminded. "When I visit the Howard house," he says, "I always take a few moments to stand in the room where he wrote all that amazing poetry and prose and try to feel a connection.

"There have been times when I've almost thought I could hear the sound of his typewriter."

Christmas
Comfort
= = = = = = = =
DECEMBER 2011

He was broke, both financially and in spirit, as that long ago holiday season approached. The father and his two young sons had moved to a rural setting, there to rebuild their lives in the wake of divorce; they by meeting new friends and tasting new country boy adventures, him struggling to carve out a living as a self-employed writer who had left behind a newspaper career.

The kids had been far more successful with the transition, oblivious to such realities that if an overdue payment didn't soon arrive from some publisher, tending the rent on the small stone cabin they called home might pose a problem.

Such was not their worry to suffer. Ages 5 and 8, theirs were days of warm innocence with no concern more serious than whether the fish would be biting along nearby Cypress Creek when the school bus delivered them home.

As the Christmas season arrived, their new home, a little

community called Comfort, began to sparkle with the colored lights strung along the eves of houses. The man and his boys followed the tradition of most of their neighbors, locating a small, well-shaped cedar sapling on a nearby hillside and taking it home for decorating.

There was the annual holiday band concert in the high school auditorium, a moonlit night of church-sponsored caroling through the town, and while there was no snow, a sudden ice storm briefly turned the landscape into a winter wonderland. And there was the steady adult hum of excited whispers about gifts bought, wrapped and hidden away.

Yet as the days too quickly passed, the man struggled with little success to find joy in the season. With the postman arriving empty-handed day after day, he worried that his first Christmas as a single father would be remembered for what it was not rather than for what he'd hoped it would be.

He had shopped carefully, his limited funds spent on small items – a puzzle book here, a toy or two there, wrapping paper and a spool of red ribbon – in hopes that once they were placed beneath the tree they would appear as more than they really were.

One evening, long after his sons were sleeping, the man sat alone in a room illuminated only by the single string of lights on the tree, pondering the meager offering of gifts. *Christmas was not just about an abundance of toys and trinkets, right? Hadn't we, as a generation, over-indulged our kids?*

So deeply in thought was he that he didn't hear the first few late night rings of the phone. When he finally answered, he heard the cheerful voice of his sister. She and her husband were thinking about making a drive through the picturesque Texas Hill Country. Okay if they stopped in for a visit?

The man had not seen them since the move and his gloom was swept away by the prospect of their coming. That in itself would be a welcomed gift.

By the time they arrived, the house had been cleaned spotless, the giddy anticipation of guests warming the day. The aroma of freshly brewed coffee wafted through the kitchen.

They hugged, talked, and laughed for some time before the brother-in-law suggested that his wife would enjoy a tour of the town. She wanted to see the boys' school, where their friends lived, view the landscape of their new life. And so they soon departed, leaving only her husband behind to rest from his long drive.

It was a few hours before they returned to find him asleep on the couch. In the corner where the Christmas tree stood, gifts in a rainbow of colored wrappings were piled. Large and small, they formed a dazzling display. Additional lights and new ornaments had been added to the tree and a tiny angel smiled down from the top of its branches.

In the years that followed, the writer-father would forge a new life, a modest degree of prosperity ultimately achieved. He is old now, his sons long since grown to manhood. Yet each year when a new chill invades the air and the holiday season approaches, he thinks back to that special time and an unexpected act of loving kindness.

To this day it is the fondest of my Christmas memories.

Annie Mae's Legacy

= = = = = = = =

SEPTEMBER 2009

There was a great urge to title this piece something cute, like "Praise The Lord and Pass the Barbecue Sauce;" maybe "Holy Smoke," or "Heaven Can Wait; I've Just Ordered the Three-Meat Platter." But, blasphemy concerns aside, that would have been a galloping injustice to the institution Annie Mae Ward, a faithful member of Huntsville, Texas' New Zion Missionary Baptist Church and barbecue cook extraordinaire, established three decades ago.

(Annie Mae died in 2010, at age 92, but the story of how she established a dining legend in her hometown is still oft-told:)

It was in the mid-'70s and her husband was helping fellow deacons with some paint and fix-up work at the church. Annie Mae suggested that he transport his barbecue grill to the New Zion parking lot so she might prepare lunch for the team of volunteers. Soon, the sweet aroma of post oak smoke wafted along the winding Montgomery Road and passersby began stopping to ask if the beef and pork ribs she was cooking were for sale.

An idea was born: New Zion elders offered to underwrite a roadside business if she wished to cook regularly. A portion of whatever she earned would go into the church coffers. For two years, the venture was a roaring success – until the city fathers visited and cited a lengthy list of licensing and health codes Annie Mae and her benefactors had innocently overlooked.

Church members quickly came to the rescue, remodeling a small frame building on a lot next door. And in 1979, the church-owned New Zion Missionary Baptist Church BBQ restaurant, fully licensed and up to code, officially opened for business. The rest, as we culinary storytellers like to say, is barbecue history.

On a recent Saturday, the church parking lot was full and across the way a lengthy line of hungry customers wound alongside the two smoky barbecue pits, waiting to enter the low-ceiling frame structure and claim one of the 60 folding chairs that line the wooden tables positioned along faded yellow walls.

There were bankers and bikers, vacationers and locals, truck drivers, lawyers and college students, diners young and old, all there to enjoy what some insist is the best food on Planet Earth. In addition to the ribs, brisket, sausage and chicken that pit master Robert Polk had been watching over since before sunrise, beans and potato salad were ready. For dessert the choices would be, as usual, buttermilk, sweet potato and pecan pie.

And now standing in the place so long occupied by Annie Mae Ward is Rev. Clinton Edison. On Sunday he'll move next door to deliver a sermon to his congregation on "The Marks of True Believers," but on this Saturday he is putting in a 10-hour day taking food orders and lending help to the three church-member employees in the kitchen.

"In Sister Ward's honor," Edison, 57, says, "we haven't changed a thing." The ingredients for the dry rub used on the meat Polk prepares and the sauce that's slathered onto the finish product are Annie Mae's recipes. ("She always told people they weren't secret; she just wasn't telling.") And her unbending house rules remain in place: No drinking, no bad language, everybody has a good time, and nobody leaves hungry.

In truth, there has been one small change. Since New Zion Missionary Baptist Church BBQ was a bit of a tongue-twister, the name of the establishment has been abbreviated over the years to simply Church BBQ.

Glowing testimonials are easy to come by. One has only to look and listen. Houston area bank president James Edrey and wife Angelia, former students at nearby Sam Houston State University, have brought their daughters – Maggie, 10; Lily 8; Hallie, 6 – for their first sample of the barbecue Mom and Dad were first exposed to as undergrads. "It was great then and it's great now," Edrey says.

Across the way, vacationing Ron Nelson and wife Joan, from Freemont, Nebraska, are good-naturedly discussing whether the buttermilk or sweet potato pie – delicacies neither had ever before tasted -- was better. "I'd had friends insist that we stop here the next time we were in Texas," Nelson says. It exceeded his expectations.

Edison estimates that the restaurant's clientele is equally divided between long-time local patrons and travelers who make the exit off Interstate 45 for lunch or dinner.

All this is accomplished by word of mouth, occasional warm mentions from food and travel journalists and a recent appearance on the Food Network's cult-followed "Diners, Drive-Ins and Dives."

"We've never advertised," Edison says. Neither do they cater. And they're open only on Thursday, Friday and Saturday, 11 a.m. to 6 p.m.

So, in a part of the world where there are more barbecue restaurants than Starbucks, what lures customers to the south side of Huntsville? What is it that would encourage diners to patiently stand in line, waiting to finally sit elbow-to-elbow with fellow barbecue lovers?

Because, for many, the quest to find the absolute best ribs, brisket, chicken and link sausage is a never-ending pursuit. It's almost like a religion.

And next door to the New Zion Missionary Baptist Church sits the Holy Grail.

* * *

(Today, the serving line remains long and the barbecue is still tasty despite the retirement of pit master Robert Polk. Doing the cooking now is Lawrence Pickett, keeping Annie Mae's legacy alive.)

Cooking the Books

= = = = = = = =

FEBRUARY 2013

Those of us who labor in the crap-shoot business of selling words for a living have heard all the fairytale stories. The ones that have people flocking to book signings by J.K. Rowling and Stephen King in such numbers that the fire marshals have to step in. The public vision is of long lines winding through the neighborhood Barnes & Noble, sweaty-palmed fans eager to get the favored author's signature on the fly leaf of his or her latest bestseller. Pretty heady stuff for one who has toiled in grim solitude to produce the 300-400 hardbacked pages that cause the welcomed celebration.

Trust me when I tell you it's not all huge crowds and smiling buyers. Me, I've spent more agonizing hours than I like to recall seated behind a stack of books in places where I wondered if someone had ordered the building evacuated. Book-buying throngs and I are total strangers.

Once, however, I did come close. Arriving for my time in the spotlight at a book fair to which numerous authors were invited to spend time meeting, greeting and signing, I was stunned to find the parking lot filled. Inside the crowd was shoulder-to-shoulder. They were waiting, I learned, to meet Benji the Dog, who, in the wake of movie fame, had "authored" a children's book and was on hand to dip a paw into a ready ink pad and leave an impression on each book purchased. As I went to a back-of-the-store office to await my turn, I was certain that some of Benji's fans might remain to meet a human writer.

When my name was announced and I strode to the table that cute little Benji had vacated, the only other person remaining in the place was a young salesman who simply shrugged his shoulders and asked if I'd like a cup of coffee. Another hard lesson learned: Never, ever follow a dog act.

So frustrated have my various publishers become over the years that they've sought "alternate venues" where I might peddle my wares. There was the showroom of an auto dealership some years back, where more tires were kicked than books bought. I've had my ego flattened in grocery stores, at a couple of chili cook-offs, in high school gyms, and more than a few sleepy retirement villages.

And each time I've sworn never again.

But what struggling author could resist the invitation of the mother-daughter team of Jo Ann and Karyn Miller to visit their Gourmet Gallery in Waco, Texas, and participate in something they were calling Cooking the Books? A lifelong sucker for outrageous puns, I quickly agreed to attend.

What I walked into was an aspiring cook's dream come true. If patrons didn't want to pick up a book they could shop for shiny pots and pans, glassware, cutlery, a variety of spices and condiments and, most important, take a cooking lesson.

From a fully operational kitchen in one corner of the store, the lesson of the day was how to prepare tasty game-day tailgating cuisine – from a healthy pulled pork wrap to meat-free nachos with walnuts and damn-the-calories brownies.

Never mind that my own culinary expertise ran no deeper than a dandy recipe for Frito Pie (mix chips and chili, stir and eat). I needed only tell a few stories about the football team whose season my book chronicled. Karyn Miller, the 47-year-old owner and her mom, a former high school home-economics teacher, promised that their audience of aspiring cooks would love it. As a bonus, Karyn's school-teaching sister, Carye Compton, was busing a group of local eighth-graders over with questions galore.

"We like to do things that are fun, different and educational," Karyn explained. Such, she says, has been the goal since the store/cooking school opened four years ago, on kitchen queen Julia Child's birthday.

All in all, it was a pleasant way to spend a lunch hour. How can you beat hanging around in a sweet-smelling kitchen, sampling new dishes and talking with nice folks? I even signed a few books.

Faith restored, I've now learned of a wine-tasting group that occasionally invites authors to attend a function they call Reading Between the Wines. I'm waiting for their call.

The Man on the Wheaties Box

= = = = = = = =

DECEMBER 2012

Never mind that he's been an ordained minister since age 18, was a two-time Olympic pole vault champion, world record holder, a 1984 presidential candidate and in every sense a bona fide American icon. Forget that he received the coveted Sullivan Award in 1951 as the nation's premier amateur athlete, is in more Halls of Fame than you can shake a stick at and has shared stages with the likes of Paul Harvey and Norman Vincent Peale, delivering motivational speeches to millions.

I still had a bone to pick with the guy.

The Rev. Bob Richards and I go back a long way, to the years between 1958 and 1972 when he was traveling the world as spokesperson for Wheaties, the Breakfast of Champions. If trivia's your thing, be aware that the man once known as the "Vaulting Vicar" and the "Pole Vaulting Parson" was the first athlete ever pictured on the front of a Wheaties box, an honor now regularly dealt the most elite of sports world achievers.

Richards' message to all us aspiring young athletes was the same: Eat your Wheaties and you, too, can grow up to be a champion.

So, as I headed to his 5,000-acre Olympian Ranch just an hour's drive south of Fort Worth, I rehearsed a question for my boyhood hero: Why, after going through enough boxes of his favorite cereal to fill a sizable warehouse, after hanging on his every word when he spoke at my high school's athletic banquet, and reading his bestselling inspirational book, *Heart of a Champion*, cover to cover, had I fallen so miserably short of my goal?

The 87-year-old Richard's smiling response was quick. "Perhaps," he said, "you've forgotten the second part of my instruction. If you'll remember, what I told kids was that a bowl of Wheaties *and* 10,000 hours of hard work would help them become champions."

Okay, point taken. Maybe I did take a few too many training breaks during my failed quest.

For Richards, today an adopted Texan, shortcuts have never been an option. The University of Illinois grad made his first Olympic team in 1948, claiming the bronze medal in London. Then, in '52 and '56 he won gold in Helsinki and Melbourne, becoming history's only two-time winner in his specialty. Even today he can vividly describe hearing the national anthem being played and a packed stadium cheering as he was acknowledged as an Olympic champion.

In truth, that was but one of the high points of his brim-full life.

"The Olympic experience was a great thrill," he says, "but, honestly, there was nothing more exciting than standing at a podium, speaking to young people, trying to motivate them to reach their own goals."

Rev. Richards' message, understand, was always about much more than good nutrition. He worked tirelessly to convince America's youth of the limitless possibilities that could result from persistence and determination. As Wheaties' spokesperson, he made an estimated 12,000 appearances. To heighten physical fitness awareness, he once bicycled from Los Angeles to New York.

He wasn't, however, General Mills' first choice to beat the drum for their breakfast cereal and newly-formed Sports Federation. First offered the position was famed University of Oklahoma football coach Bud Wilkinson, whose teams had just established a national record of 47 consecutive wins. Turning down the offer to enter the political arena, Wilkinson made a suggestion: "You should call Bob Richards. He's the greatest public speaker in America."

That's how Richards came into my life and Wheaties became a breakfast table staple.

Today, his pace has finally slowed. Retired from public speaking, he had recently sold his West Texas horse ranch after 43 years and moved with wife Joan to nearby Waco where they could more closely watch the latest family pole vaulter's progress. Grandson Riley, 13, has already cleared 12 feet. "His dad, Brandon," Richards points out, "held the national high school record in the event for 14 years and ultimately had a best of 18-2." Son Tommy cleared 17-4, Paul, 16-4, and Bobby, 17-6.

"Add my best of 15-6," the proud father/grandfather says, quickly reminding that his height was accomplished in the days before the invention of the flexible fiberglass poles that now launch vaulters to two-story heights, "and we surely hold the world family record in the event."

And so the remarkable legacy continues. Recently, he said, Wheaties had produced a box featuring a historical timeline of the cereal and its glowing parade of champions. Among those featured, of course, was Richards.

All forgiven, I headed for my neighborhood grocery.

* * *

(Now 90, Bob Richards still makes his home in Waco, where he watches over two golf courses that he's purchased.)

The Legend

= = = = = = = =

AUGUST 2010

Even as the ambulance hurried away from the parking lot of Wynnewood, Oklahoma's Full House Tavern on that Labor Day weekend in 2008, there were those convinced that the whole frightening thing was just another one of Billy Mays' elaborate tricks. What bystanders wouldn't learn until later was that en route to the hospital, the legendary sportsman's heart stopped beating.

In fact, attending paramedics had good reason to believe that the country's greatest barroom shuffleboard player, in the throes of a full-blown heart attack, had played his last game. Even as they attempted to resuscitate him, the odds were they would soon pronounce him dead.

Shows what they knew about Roadhouse Billy.

Four days later, with newly implanted stints clearing blocked arteries, the 72-year-old year-old Table Shuffleboard Association Hall of Famer checked himself out of the hospital against the advice of doctors and was back in business, taking bets, performing trick shots and pocketing the money of competitors half his age.

"What I found out," he sagely notes as he puffs on a Pall Mall, "is that dying is easy; it's living that's hard."

Daymon Runyon couldn't have dreamed up this guy. He's shuffleboard's rock star, colorful, cagey, and cocky. For most of his adult life he's traveled the American backroads, earning his living in beer joints and cocktail lounges throughout the U.S. and a half dozen Canadian provinces.

Understand, we're not talking the kind of fun-in-the-sun shuffleboard played in retirement communities and aboard cruise ships. Mays' game is the England-born pub sport played with circular weights that are lagged along a 22-foot, highly polished maplewood table. It's a game of delicate touch and war-like strategy. And Billy Mays has been its master craftsman for a half century.

He's been crowned world champion 25 times. If barroom shuffleboard was an Olympic sport, he'd be up to his horn-rimmed glasses in gold medals. "I've always believed that every man born has something that he can do better than anyone in the world," he says. "I'm lucky. I found that thing I can do better than anybody."

And with that he's off on a trip down memory lane: Beating movie idol Rock Hudson in a series of games in North Hollywood back in the early '60s; being hired to teach legendary con man, hustler Titanic Thompson how to play; matching talent and wit with long-time rival Granville Humphrey for 60 straight hours in Oklahoma City; a 90-day visit in California during which he won $120,000; and playing against guys with nicknames like Suicide Ray, Cable Car Denny, Blind John and Wacky Dan.

Hesitant to tally his career earnings, he only admits that he's probably won a dollar for every mile he's traveled. Suffice it to say his endless search for the next game has spread over several million miles. You do the math.

And when he's not bent over the shuffleboard table, he's got a laundry list of bar tricks that'll clean your pockets. Want to bet he can't blow a dime from the edge of the table into a nearby beer glass? Trust me: don't. He estimates that one alone has supplemented his income by a hundred grand over the years.

None of which would have happened had he not injured his back while roughnecking on an off-shore oil rig back in the late '50s. Limping home to Dallas, broke and wearing a back brace, he was sitting in a local beer joint on an evening when Humphrey, at the time the premier shuffleboard player in the country, invited him to play. As Humphrey's partner, the 20-year-old Mays pocketed $40. "The next morning, I was standing outside the bar, waiting for it to open. I played shuffleboard until it closed at midnight. Did that day after day," he recalls.

In three months he was the best player in town and went on the road to expand his reputation. From Michael's Bar in Philly to The Barn in Costa Mesa, California ("Appearing Nightly: The Costa Mesa Police Department," a wall sign once proclaimed), he sought out the best players and defeated them. Johnny Carson invited him to do his trick shots on the "Tonight Show" and *Sports Illustrated* profiled him. He's just guessing, but says he's probably won 800 tournaments during his lengthy career.

"While he's doubtless the greatest player ever," says shuffleboard-hooked Dallas lawyer Robert Hoffman, "he's an even better teacher. You make a list of the top players today and virtually all of them have taken lessons from Billy."

These days, Mays admits, his game isn't what it once was. A mild stroke in 2003 made it necessary for the natural right-hander to learn to play left-handed. And, oh yeah, he's been blind in one eye since age nine. Then, there's that heart attack thing. Now he plays only two or three days a week and doesn't travel as widely.

"Truth is," he admits, "I'm probably not *the* best anymore. But I'm still one of them."

They held a tournament at Volcano's Sports Bar & Grill in Hurst, Texas, recently and Billy Mays played. Guess who won.

* * *

(Mays died in 2015 at age 78. Volcano's hosted a Billy Mays Memorial Shuffleboard Tournament in his honor. There were lots of old stories, laughter, and a few tears. His daughter, Brenda, arrived with the urn containing his ashes and placed it on the bar. Billy would have liked that.)

Of Brothers and Baseball

= = = = = = = =

JUNE 2009

Long before it was swallowed up in a firestorm of multi-million dollar contract negotiations, player strikes, steroid controversies, television control and, Lord help us, aluminum bats for the Little Leaguers, baseball was our warmly-embraced national pastime. Like ol' Casey Stengel used to say, you can look it up.

Peanuts, popcorn and Cracker Jacks, daytime World Series, reading the box scores and trading bubble gum cards. From the sandlots to big league stadiums, it was the Rite of Spring that beckoned us one and all.

For my money the game was never a more treasured part of the American culture than in those bygone days when town ball was the order of the day. No fancy uniforms or manicured fields. No trophies for all who played. Just a bunch of marginally talented guys from one community playing against those from the town down the road, briefly dismissing Depression doldrums with nine innings of Sunday afternoon fun.

That's the way it was in the heyday of the Waukegan, Illinois, Stanczak brothers – all 10 of them – when they ruled amateur baseball in the suburban Chicago area. Same in the verdant Texas Hill Country community of Hye where the team composed of the nine Deike brothers was the local rage.

Never heard of them? Or of the time they met to play for the All-Brothers Baseball Championship? Pull up a chair.

The game was the brainstorm of a Texas coffee salesman who, while making his rounds, overheard Hye General Store owner Fritz Deike bragging that he had enough sons to make up the little town's baseball team. Thus was born a promotional idea that sent the salesman in search of another family team he might match against the Texans.

He found it in Waukegan where the Stanczaks had a reputation for taking on all comers. They'd already defeated one all-brothers team from faraway Hawk Springs, Wyoming, in a 1929 home-and-home series. You bet, they'd be happy to play the Deike brothers – anytime, any place.

Understand the Stanczaks, ranging in age from 20 to 40, took their baseball seriously.   Fact is, third baseman Michael, who would ultimately become a Catholic priest, saw his evangelical calling briefly delayed when he opted to skip his first ordination ceremony because a game had been scheduled. The Archbishop might not have been pleased but, hey, history shows that Father Mike hit a game-winning double that day.

The brothers had begun playing baseball as youngsters in a vacant field near their Waukegan home. And, as they grew older, they joined various neighborhood teams. Ultimately, they decided it was time to combine efforts and field their own family team. Their reputation grew rapidly as they routinely won local amateur league and tournament championships.

In 1933, when they defeated the Knights of Lithuania for the Lake County championship, a crowd of 1,200 was on hand.

Down in Texas, the crowds that watched the Diekes play teams from nearby Kerrville, Fredricksburg, and Grapetown, weren't nearly so large. Their makeshift home field was their dad's goat pasture. Yet the team's reputation was nothing to sneeze at. Pitcher Marvin had a wicked fastball and could hit the ball a mile. Levi, who served as the community's postmaster, was the best shortstop in Blanco County.

The Deike team ranged in age from 14-year-old left fielder Victor to 34-year-old right fielder Edwin.

It was in August of 1935 that the two teams, given new uniforms and $600 for travel expenses by the Corpus Christi-based Nueces Coffee Company, set out for Wichita, Kansas' Lawrence Stadium where the ballyhooed game would be played. The Stanczaks traveled in a rented bus, the Deikes made the trip in two Model A's.

The game matched two immigrant nationalities and starkly different lifestyles: the Polish Stanczaks against the German Deikes, city folks vs. country boys, North against South.

And, once again, the Stanczaks proved themselves the best. The Deikes, competing in a night game under lights for the first time, took an early 3-0 lead, but the Stanczaks quickly responded with seven runs as fielding errors plagued the nervous Texans. The

Waukegan brothers went on to win, 11-5.

Thus it is their team picture that today is displayed in Cooperstown's Baseball Hall of Fame.

In time, age and adult responsibilities brought an end to both legendary teams. Father Mike went on to pastor a church in Milwaukee while brother Joseph held public office in Chicago for 39 years. Edward and Joseph became co-owners of the Chicago Yellow Cab Company.

While Frederick Deike lived out his life in Hye after taking over operation of his father's general store and Levi stayed for a record-setting 64-year tenure as postmaster, most members of the team eventually moved on to greater opportunities in larger Texas cities.

Today the Stanczaks and Deikes are all gone, leaving behind only the faint memory of that long ago glorious night in Wichita – when the sport of baseball reigned as king of all pastimes.

Move Over, Roswell

======

MAY 2010

To the skeptics, the stories always seem to begin something like this: "See, me 'n Betty Lou, we were riding home just before midnight, and from outta nowhere this big ol' cigar-shaped object with blinking lights comes flying over... It was like nothing I'd ever seen... came straight toward us until it stopped and just kinda hovered for a minute. Then, lickety-split, it was gone."

According to the Fort Collins, Colorado, based Mutual UFO Network, a national organization of investigators who keep tabs on this kind of thing, such reports come in throughout the United States at a rate of approximately 200 per month. That, real or imagined, is a lot of strange goings-on up in the Wild Blue Yonder.

And, you should know, the phenomenon is nothing new. It's been going on for over 100 years, at least back to an April 1897 morning when, according to one of the country's leading newspapers, an "airship" sailed directly over the Aurora, Texas, town square and crashed into Judge J.F. Proctor's windmill, exploding into a hail storm of aluminum-looking debris that was said to have scattered over several acres. And that, bear in mind, was almost a decade before Orville and Wilbur Wright got their rickety airplane off the ground at Kitty Hawk; before the Hindenburg-like blimps were being flown and a heckuva long time before the famous 1947 Roswell UFO crash story became the gold standard of all flying saucer tales.

Yet right there on the front page of the *Dallas Morning News*, written by correspondent S.E. Haydon, was a story describing the crash that allegedly occurred in the small community just west of Fort Worth. Not only did Haydon dutifully make note of the fact the explosion wrecked Judge Proctor's windmill, water tank and destroyed his flower garden, but he detailed the fact that the airship's child-sized pilot was found among the wreckage and buried in the local cemetery the following day. The gravesite was marked with a small rock headstone that featured a crudely carved image of "a cigar-shaped airship with three circular windows."

Now, we're way past fuzzy blinking lights in the sky and into "X Files" territory.

And today, over a century later, the jury remains out on what did or didn't occur in the Texas hamlet. In one corner you have those who believe that Haydon, a man apparently fond of tall tales and bored with the lack of any real news in Aurora, just made up the whole thing. Others, however, tend to at least believe "something" happened that day. As late as 1973, an aviation writer named Bill Case, tracked down local resident G.C. Curley, 98 at the time, who recalled visiting the crash site as a child and seeing "the torn up body" of the ship's pilot.

And for years the small headstone stood in place at the space traveler's alleged burial site. But, after a photo of it ran with Case's article, someone stole it, now making it difficult to even be certain where the grave was located. Members of the Aurora Cemetery Association did ultimately allow a historical marker relating the story of the crash and burial to be placed at the graveyard entrance but have stubbornly balked at all requests to re-locate the grave and exhume any remains.

And so, the ancient mystery has endured, mostly forgotten by all but the UFO believers who still arrive to get a first-hand look at the picturesque Aurora landscape.

Legendary investigative reporter/author Jim Marrs, who has spent a lifetime skeptically poking around in things spooky and unexplained, says he remains "undecided" about the whole truth of the Aurora crash. Still, he quickly points out that it was not an isolated event but, rather, the climax of months of "sightings" throughout the U.S. and Canada.

Near Tacoma, Washington, two fishermen reported watching the landing of a metallic, cigar-shaped craft that was 20 yards in length. In Sacramento, California, over 200 people witnessed a cylindrical object with bright, pulsating lights sailing over the city. Within a few days people in Oakland and San Francisco were filing similar reports. In time sightings were being reported in Illinois, Iowa, Kansas, Arkansas, Missouri and, finally, Texas.

"What pushed me off dead center," Marrs says, "was finally seeing the entire front page of that 1897 edition of the *Morning News* in which the Aurora story appeared. On that day alone there were 16 stories about UFO sightings, reported by correspondents from as far south as Austin to parts of Oklahoma in the north. The lead story, in fact, was not the one about the Aurora crash but, rather, one datelined Stephenville, Texas, headlined "The Great Aerial Wanderer," which told of numerous residents seeing strange things in the sky.

This, he carefully reminds, was back in horse-and-buggy days when long-distance communication was still in its infancy and achingly slow; a time when it was highly unlikely that a nationwide group of goofballs could hatch a hoax of such magnitude.

Most interesting, the stories that flourished throughout the West, Midwest and South for months, suddenly ended following the report of the Aurora crash. "I'm convinced there was *something* unnatural flying around in the Texas skies at the time and am now inclined to believe something did indeed happen in Aurora," he says.

Correspondent Haydon would, no doubt, be pleased.

Thank You, Mr. Carnegie

= = = = = = = =

AUGUST 2011

Those of us of a fading generation remember them well, stone beacons that lured us through their doorways to the fantasies and great adventures they housed. Long before there was 24-7 cable television, all manner of electronic gadgetry and endless organized activities, we filled the idle times of our youth with books borrowed from the local library.

We read *Treasure Island* and *Black Beauty*, were introduced to fascinating characters, real and imagined, from Tom Sawyer and Robin Hood to Daniel Boone and Davy Crockett – simply after showing a free-for-nothing library card that enabled us to pick what we wished to take home on two-week loan.

Such were my reflections recently as I made my way back to my heartland, there to celebrate a good friend's birthday.

This year, the old two-story limestone Carnegie Public Library in little Ballinger, Texas (pop. 3,670), is 100 years old, still providing its services to the 700 or so patrons who visit monthly to browse among its 15,000 fiction and non-fiction titles.

And today, as it was back when I first found my way to its seemingly endless maze of shelves, the man we all have to thank is a Scotland-born industrialist whose vast fortune was exceeded only by his generosity. Of course I didn't know Andrew Carnegie personally, inasmuch as he died two decades before I was even born, but, Lordy, do I owe him. As do millions of others who first developed their habit of reading with visits to public libraries named in his honor.

Time was when Carnegie libraries were the rule rather than the exception in United States cities large and small. At one time there were 1,689 of them from coast to coast, each funded over a 30-year period with grants from the generous and foresighted steel magnate. As he once observed, "A public library is the never failing spring in the desert."

In 1908 he wrote a check for the $17,500 needed to build the first library I would ever visit. Other larger cities got considerably more. A few years earlier, for instance, New York City had received a $5,202,621 Carnegie grant to build libraries throughout Manhattan, Staten Island, Brooklyn, Queens and the Bronx. Dallas got $76,000 to build its first public library. The first U.S. Carnegie library, located in Fairfield, Iowa, was built in 1893, at a whopping cost of $40,000.

It was, in fact, in the small towns that they flourished, standing as the centerpieces of the community. Remember Sinclair Lewis' classic novel, *Main Street*? His heroine was the Carnegie librarian, her fictional workplace the symbol of the social awareness she struggled to bring to the local residents.

In Ballinger, it has been much the same.

Local historian Janice Routh recalls when the library not only dispensed books but during World War I was the place where Red Cross volunteers gathered to roll bandages to be forwarded to American troops. Later, its upstairs served as the World War II home of the Army and Navy Club where training cadets from the nearby flight school gathered for social events. And before the public school had its own cafeteria, students were served a noon meal prepared in the library's kitchen.

History, this place has.

When I first visited it in the early '50s, it seemed a much larger and daunting place than it appears today, the steps leading to its front door far steeper and more demanding, the ceilings higher than in any building I'd ever seen. And I'd have guessed the number of books it contained to be somewhere in the millions.

Such was the view through 12-year-old eyes.

Now, over a half century later, computers have replaced the old card catalog, a younger generation comes not only for books but videos and free access to the Internet. Librarian Julie Gray constantly searches for new and inventive ways to fund needed repairs to the old building, purchase more books and provide new programs for her patrons. "This is such a wonderful place," she says. "I began coming here as a little girl, always amazed that there were so many books in one place. To me it's still magical."

Today, the Carnegie libraries like the one she watches over are fading into history. Many, having served their purpose, have been demolished, replaced by more modern facilities. Some, still standing, have been converted into museums. In her native Texas, Gray points out, there were once 32 Carnegie libraries. Today, Ballinger's is one of just four still active in the state.

According to Theodore Jones, author of *Carnegie Libraries Across America*, by 1997 only 772 functioning Carnegie libraries remained in the U.S. No doubt, that number has continued to dwindle.

As we neared the check-out desk at the end of my sentimental journey, Gray pointed out that it was the same one that has been used throughout the century-long life of the library. "When you checked out books as a boy," she said, "you stood right here."

Back then, when Ms. Watkins was the librarian, seated behind it and stamping the return date into the books I was borrowing, it seemed so much bigger.

* * *

(The aging library marches on, with ongoing renovation and a continued determination to serve its patrons.)

Hinterland
High School
= = = = = = = =

MAY 2012

Admittedly, as one who happily thought he'd met his high school foreign language requirement by finally passing Algebra I, I'm hardly the ideal spokesman to address today's troubling state of our children's education.

Still, it doesn't require dazzling insight or a celestial IQ to know that our nation's public schools are in turmoil. Just read the papers: Budget woes, testing problems, overburdened and underpaid teachers, discipline run amok and crammed classrooms. The Three Rs have lost the battle to TAKS. And don't even get me started on this new philosophy that no child should ever fail, lest he or she suffer irreparable emotional damage.

All of which begs the thundering question of what we're to do.

Perhaps it might be time well spent for the academic Big Thinkers to pay a visit to Central Texas and the tiny office of Superintendent Scot Kelley, 46, who, for the past five years, has watched over the Penelope Independent School District and its 175 kindergarten through 12th grade students. Pardon the nostalgia, but his is the kind of workable school system I remember.

Though his district ranks as one of the poorest in the far-spread Texas system, with only bare minimum property tax revenue to draw from, the Penelope ISD appears to be managing quite well. Kids are learning from the 22 classroom teachers, they graduate and some go on to college. A few even return. Audra Osborne, the Homecoming Queen and a high achiever a few years ago, recently earned her degree at Texas Tech before coming back to her hometown, population 200, to teach English.

The majority of her students, life-long residents, arrive from farms and ranches spread across the 55-square mile school district. Others are more recent arrivals, enrolled by parents grown weary of inner city social and educational shortcomings, who made the move to the sanity and simple pleasures of small-town life. The enrollment is diverse – Anglo, African-American, Hispanic – and the curriculum on par with far larger schools.

The greatest difference is the student-teacher ratio. "We may have a physics class with just five students," Kelley notes. "Whatever the subject, there is a great deal of one-on-one teaching going on. Nobody gets lost in the shuffle. Our teachers know every child in school and what each's individual needs are."

If there is a course that a student wants to take but isn't available at Penelope High, arrangements are in place for live interactive video instruction from nearby Hill College.

"Here," the superintendent says, "it is our job to look beyond what we might not have and find ways to *make* things happen."

Despite the fact the school has no stage on which to practice, its one-act play participants have won championships. So has its six-man football team and members of its Future Farmers of America. Annually, students fare well in academic competitions. Never mind that there's no tennis court in Penelope. The school's team is driven to nearby Waco by its coach for after-school practice.

Welcome to education in the hinterland, where a stubborn make-do approach is the order of every day.

If the trend holds, of the 15 seniors in this year's class a third of them will seek higher learning. "There was a time when a number of our kids didn't really know how to get into college," Kelley points out. "Now, we help them every step of the way. We make sure they've taken all the required subjects, help them fill out applications, and our teachers often donate their time to drive them to visit nearby college campuses."

For the superintendent and his teachers, education is far more than a morning bell-to-afternoon dismissal proposition.

When the school day ends, Kelley switches from his role of administrator to tutor. Some who have come to him for help were ex-students from bygone days who, for whatever reason, failed to earn their diploma.

In one case he recalls, a 24-year-old had failed to pass the TAKS test in his senior year and, with a young daughter about to enroll, wanted to be able to tell her he was a high school graduate. For six months Kelley worked with him. When the test was finally taken and passed last summer, it was his tutor who presented the proud young father his diploma.

"That," says Kelley, "was something very special to me."

Reunion

\=\=\=\=\=\=\=\=\=

JUNE 2010

In the trappings of adulthood, it seems, we have become so eternally busy with thoughts of tomorrow – career ladders to climb, mortgage payments coming due, concern over the kids' college funds – that there is little time left to reflect on the past. We allow ourselves no place to retreat, even briefly, from the weary unrest of new wars, old politics and endless economic concerns; precious few opportunities to escape to gentler, simpler times when worries were few, the music sweet and young friends were forever.

As they say, nostalgia's not what it used to be.

Such were my thoughts recently as I drove toward Austin, Texas, there to join fellow old geezers who had been invited to participate in an evening ceremony that was to be held in the stadium where the annual Texas high school state track and field championships were being conducted. Celebrating its 100th year, the meet's officials had decided to honor the schools which had won the most titles during its history. My alma mater had won seven. A lifetime ago I had been fortunate enough to have been a small part of that. And as I drove, memories, a half-century old, flooded back. As if by some gentle stroke of whimsy, I could hear the rockabilly sounds of Elvis again, remember the powerful pout of actor James Dean, the names of old girlfriends, favored teachers and coaches, and the thrill of being a part of a team made up of people who have, over so many years, remained important to me.

If you are among those certain that athletics are over-emphasized and nothing more than a distraction to academic pursuit, read no farther. It is my unwavering opinion that all those lessons learned in long afternoons of practice, then in the competitive arena, gave purpose and direction to our young lives. We learned of goal-setting and sportsmanship, winning and losing, and the rewards of contributing to a team effort. For many of us, those lessons provided the opportunity to continue our education at the college level. In my house, and in those of most of my teammates, the option was simple: No athletic scholarship, no college.

And so in time we went our separate ways – off to the University of Texas, SMU, Oklahoma, Rice, Texas Tech and hometown Abilene Christian, just to name a few – yet stayed in touch.

We are all old now, gray-haired and more slow-moving. Once carefree teenagers, we are grandfathers today, dutifully attending sports competitions of a new generation. Sadly, some of us are gone after grim battles far more serious than simply striving to win a gold medal. But for those who remain, invited to regroup and gather in front of a crowd of 20,000 and once again be called Abilene High School Eagles, it was a time-travel respite that for a moment made all the ills of the world disappear. For a brief snapshot of time we were kids again, reunited to joke, embrace unashamedly... and remember.

As best I recall none of those gathered had been the product of childhood privilege, all the sons of hard-working, nine-to-five parents who were supportive, loving and proud. And without exception they had grown into adult successes, becoming doctors, teachers, and lawyers, CEOs, artists and coaches.

Their journeys began back when, as kids, they did their best to run faster, jump higher and throw farther than the competition they faced on those charmed spring weekends. I can still see Dr. Charles McCook, determinedly anchoring our mile relay to victory despite a leg pain that would later be diagnosed as a fractured fibula; insurance executive Larry Rhodes setting the state record in the 880-yard run and old buddy Gerald Cumby reigning as the state pole vault champion in a time when poles were stiff and didn't catapult their carriers to two-story heights. Bobby Johnson, the state's best high hurdler, is retired now, still married to his high school sweetheart. Andy Springer might today be a successful businessman, but I remember him best as our school record-holder in the long jump. And James Blackwood, son of the local fire marshal, has, at last count, coached no fewer than 17 Olympians.

Their names will mean little to most. Their youthful achievements are forgotten save for us who were there as witnesses, now surpassed by swifter, stronger athletes who have followed. But to me they remain special. That's the purpose of memories.

And so we gathered, uncomfortably nodding to modest applause for bygone accomplishments, then quickly retreated into the stands, back into the real world, giving way to a new and excited group of young athletes who would record far better times and distances than those of the ancient '50s and '60s.

And as we did so, it occurred to me that an occasional sip of nostalgia has a sweet and refreshing taste. If nothing else, it serves to remind us of who we were and how it charted the course to who we would become.

Too Many Trophies?

= = = = = = = = =

AUGUST 2012

In my grandson's cluttered bedroom there are enough trophies, medals, ribbons and good deed certificates to satisfy a young athlete's growing ego for a lifetime. He's 12. About him, as he lies on his bed doing homework or watching SportsCenter, he is surrounded by material evidence that he has enjoyed and excelled on the playing field. There are trophies for tournaments won in baseball, league championships in basketball and soccer. Some simply signify that he attended practice dutifully, put on a uniform on game day and was part of the team. There are Olympic-sized medals he has returned home with from summer sports camps.

Welcome to the Trophy for All age. Don't misunderstand; it delights me to see the sparkle in his eye as he steps forward to receive an award. I was among those applauding mightily when his first home run ball went out of the park and when goals found their way into the back of the net. Still, as I survey the shiny signs of achievement he has collected, it is difficult to determine which signify true excellence and those presented for simply participating. And I wonder if the standard for today's sports world prizes sends the proper message. The question, admittedly, is born of an ancient lament that things were different back in the day.

One need only look at the proud athletic history of Abilene to grasp the notion that the most valid spoils go to the winners. It has had its Team of the Century state championships in football and baseball back in the days when only that team with the best district record qualified for the playoffs. It won state track championships by adhering to the rule that only the best of its athletes advance through district and regional competitions to reach the state meet. Such are achievements not all can attain. By its nature, athletic competition was, since the ancient days of the Rome Empire, assigned the task of saluting its winners above all others. For the also-ran there was scant glory.

All of which is a bit old-fashioned and hard-lined in the minds of a growing generation that has taken a position that turning away from such emphasis on victory is more vital to society than won-lost records.

Today, in schoolboy athletics, it is no longer just the district champion that is given the singular honor of advancing into the playoffs. In a nod to enrollment fairness, the University Interscholastic League has even broken things into divisions, large and small. Realignment occurs so regularly that it is difficult to keep up with who plays who every couple of years. They have made the changes in the name of economic sanity and fair play and it is difficult to argue against their dictates.

Doesn't mean, however, that we old fuss-budgets have to

embrace it.

The arguments, like baseball's designated hitter rule and NFL's tie-breaker format, have no clear-cut winners. Is it fair for a high school with less enrollment to be matched against one with greater resources? Can a financially encumbered school be expected to compete against those with bulging pockets and big budgets? Where can the line of true fairness be drawn to assure that legitimate champions are declared?

Will, under today's new philosophy, we ever again really know which team is best?

On the horizon near my home is the Cedar Hill water tower which proudly bears the words "State Champions 5A, Div.II, 2006." In a perfect world would the townspeople prefer that the footnote wasn't there?

Think back to a simpler time, the mid-'50s, when neighboring Breckenridge, oil rich and blessed with outstanding players, had barely enough kids in school to qualify for competition at the Class AAA level. Yet in the non-district season they took on larger Class AAAA powerhouses like Abilene and Wichita Falls and won. In fact, in 1954, as UIL authorities were contemplating demoting them to Class AA, the Bucs won state in their larger classification. Along the way they also defeated Abilene High, which went on to claim the AAAA title that year. Neither advanced to the playoffs by finishing second or third in their district. It was a winner-take-all time in Texas schoolboy history. And it seemed right.

And now progress has reduced that simple formula to faded memory. It is a change that still takes some getting used to, this business of more champions, more participation, more feel good trophies to be handed out at season's end.

Recently, at my four-year-old granddaughter's dance recital she seemed less than pleased at the conclusion of the evening's performance. She had, at least in ol' granddad's judgment, done well. Hadn't she heard the approving applause for her and the other dancers? Why the long face?

"I wanted to get a trophy," she explained, speaking out for a new generation.

Thurber, Texas, Pop. 4

= = = = = = = =

SEPTEMBER 2011

If one listens carefully, the winds speak in haunting whispers of times past. Soft and wistful, almost as if quietly pleading, calling back faded memories. That, in most instances, is all that is left of the thousands of ghost towns across the American landscape.

Yet in a lifetime of wandering backroads, I have been drawn to them; places with fascinating histories and lyrical names like Terlingua and Salt Flat, Glory, Thalia and Chalk Mountain. And Thurber.

In many cases they are no longer even dots on the map, their residents gone, victims of economic hard times, plagues, tornadoes, fires, and floods. Or, in the case of Thurber, Texas, the closing of the mines.

Back in the late 1800s and early 1900s, when its coal mines were fueling locomotives and its brick production provided streets for major cities throughout the Southwest, its population climbed as high as 10,000, making it the largest city between Fort Worth and El Paso. In its glory days, Thurber was an ethnic melting pot, where home-grown workers labored alongside immigrants who arrived from as many as 20 foreign countries to chase the American Dream.

Today, however, as travelers speed by on Interstate 20, 75 miles west of Fort Worth, they glimpse only an old landmark smokestack that stubbornly stands sentry. It and a cemetery with over 1,000 headstones remain as the most visible proof of what once was.

It was a "company town," owned lock, stock and mine shafts by the Texas & Pacific Coal Company. It had schools taught by no fewer than 17 teachers, churches for all denominations, the only library in the county, a 650-seat opera house, general store, fire station, post office, weekly newspaper, hotel and row upon row of small frame homes where its workers and their families resided.

Folks worked – and played—hard. When they weren't digging in the mines, they gathered around the town bandstand for concerts, looked forward to that annual summer weekend when a touring circus came to town, swam and fished in the man-made Big Lake nearby. Their semi-pro baseball team drew large crowds and won the 1896 Texas state championship. Workers frequently enjoyed a few cool ones at the local Snake Saloon once the work day ended.

They deserved it, considering the fact they were producing 3,000 tons of bituminous coal and 80,000 bricks per day.

Historians insist that it was the first community in the nation to be totally unionized, every working resident a dues-paying member of the United Mine Workers.

Born in 1886, Thurber officially died in 1936. The arrival of the Oil Boom killed it. Suddenly it was more efficient to fuel trains with oil rather than coal. Oil-based asphalt replaced brick on road constructions. The mines closed and the inhabitants scattered in search of new work. Most of the town was razed. The frame homes were sold for $40 each to anyone willing to haul them away.

And, yes, there are the ghost stories. Like the oft-told tale of a weeping woman, clad in white, who wanders nearby Cemetery Hill, said to still be mourning the drowning death of her son almost a century ago. Or a sad-faced little girl in a summer dress, carrying a parasol, who is said to have mysteriously appeared in the background of photographs taken by long ago residents.

One of the few buildings that remains is the old red brick general store. Today it is the Smokestack Restaurant, a home-cooking way-stop that is owned and operated by Andrea Bennett, who resides nearby in a 100-year-old house which was once the home to the company doctor. Since the 2000 death of her husband Randy, a descendent of Texas & Pacific superintendent Carroll Bennett, she and her three sons are the only full-time Thurber residents.

"People who stop," Bennett says, "love to look at the old pictures we have on the restaurant walls, showing the town as it once was. And they always ask questions." She likes that. It keeps the memories alive.

* * *

(For more information on Thurber's history, including fascinating artifacts and photos, visit the W.K. Gordon Center in Thurber. The museum is open Tuesday-Saturday 10 a.m. to 4 p.m. and Sunday 1–4 p.m. It's more than worth the $4 admission.)

Burning in the Wind

= = = = = = = =

DECEMBER 2007

The historical landscape of West Texas is littered with colorful tales of remarkable deeds and doers, the rise of down-and-outers to mega fortune, local products who have gone on to celebrity status in endeavors ranging from White House politics and movie stardom to great athletic and academic achievement; the evil lawless and those who heroically pursued them.

By best account, however, there's been but one book burning.

It is said to have occurred in 1925, after a gifted and gentle Texas author and educator named Dorothy Scarborough wrote a novel that on one hand earned her national applause and the other received scathing response from the community leaders of the town in which her book was set.

First published anonymously, *The Wind* told of a teenage orphan from Virginia who arrived in Sweetwater in the drought-plagued 1880s to live with her cousins, only to be slowly driven to insanity, murder and finally suicide by the bleak, wind-blown world into which she'd settled. As the Mount Carmel, Texas-born Scarborough wrote: "The wind was the cause of it all. The sand, too, had a share in it, and human beings were involved, but the wind was the primal force..."

So powerful and successful was the novel that it was judged one of the best published that year and was later made into in a well-received silent film starring the legendary Lillian Gish. None of which impressed the folks in Sweetwater, where Scarborough had spent several years of her childhood.

Reacting to the fact the book had been published anonymously, the first wave of local outrage suggested that some Eastern hack, without the slightest knowledge of the culture and geography, had written the melodramatic novel. Angry letters were sent to the publisher and newspapers throughout Texas, blasting *The Wind* and its author who apparently had lacked the courage to assign his or her name.

Leading the assault was Judge R.C. Crane, a Sweetwater civic leader and founder of the West Texas Historical Association. In letters to the book's publisher as well as the *Dallas Morning News*, he insisted that its author had fallen woefully short of an honest portrayal of his hometown and its history – not to mention that the wind hardly blew as much as the book suggested.

And then, angered locals who had purchased the book, gathered in front of the Nolan County courthouse and set their copies aflame.

You can't buy the kind of publicity the ongoing uproar generated.

The publisher's plan to release the book without the author's name – a tactic that had previously been successful with another writer's novel – had worked like clockwork. Sales increased to a point where a second printing was soon ordered. This time, however, the book bore Dorothy Scarborough's name.

Well before the second printing, she had written a firm, polite response to Judge Crane's tirade that had been published in the *Morning News*. According to an article written by Dr. Sylvia Grider in the 1986 *West Texas Historical Association Year Book,* Scarborough methodically refuted the judge's criticisms, finally asking, "Has the West Texas wind got on your nerves, Mr. Crane, and the sand blinded you to the difference between a novel and a historical treatise?"

Dr. Grider, a longtime Scarborough scholar, writes that the author's response was an ice-breaker. At the height of her book's success, she was invited to Sweetwater to speak. In a classic bit of irony, the author arrived at the height of one of the most vicious sandstorms the region had experienced in years. And when she accepted Crane's invitation to tour the countryside so that he might point out the beauty she'd overlooked, they were caught in a blue norther so severe that it made their return to town difficult. If Scarborough hadn't already won her battle with the judge, she did so when she presented him a signed copy of *The Wind*. By trip's end, Dr. Grider writes, "Scarborough's visit to Sweetwater turned out to be a triumphal tour."

Though still considered by many scholars as one of the premier Texas novels ever written, *The Wind* is now but a whisper on the literary landscape. Its last publication was a paperback edition almost three decades ago. Yet there is little question Scarborough pointed the way for the modern day likes of Larry McMurtry and Cormac McCarthy..

She taught literature and creative writing at Baylor, where she'd earlier earned her B.A. (and later an honorary doctor of literature), and at Columbia, where she earned her doctorate. She also studied at Oxford. And though none of her other books created the stir of *The Wind*, she continued to write, the theme of her fiction and non-fiction, short stories and poetry generally focusing on the plight of early day Texas women.

While she called New York home in the years before her death in 1935, Scarborough made one final trip back to Texas. She is buried in Waco's Oakwood Cemetery, where, it is said, the wind only gently blows.

Santa's Ghostwriter

= = = = = = = =

DECEMBER 2012

Today's literary marketplace, you realize, is bursting at the seams with them; autobiographies of pop culture icons and politicians, sports heroes and business geniuses. Want to know what makes today's headline-makers tick? Just pay a visit to your local library or bookstore.

And while these celebrities can sing, dance, manage fortunes, run like the wind and deliver bang-up speeches, when it comes to the business of authorship they regularly turn to hired Boswells for the heavy lifting. They call them ghostwriters.

Few in the field have enjoyed the success of Jeff Guinn, an oft-honored author who reluctantly took on the task of telling the remarkable story of one of the world's most beloved personalities, a man who has reigned supreme in the hearts and minds of millions. When his editor first pitched the novel idea, Jeff said no thanks.

This, he swears, is how he was finally won over: It was his day off from duties as book editor for the *Fort Worth Star-Telegram* and he was busily trying to make points with the lady of the house by vacuuming the den when he heard the words, *"You're right to believe in me."* Santa Claus, of all people, had beckoned Guinn's subconscious and he rushed immediately to his upstairs office and began to write.

Four hours later he returned to find smoke billowing from the vacuum cleaner, its motor burned beyond repair. Two things were certain. He'd have to buy his wife a new appliance and he would write a fact-and-fiction "autobiography" of Jolly Ol' Saint Nick.

That was four Christmas-related books – *The Autobiography of Santa Claus, How Mrs. Claus Saved Christmas, The Great Santa Search* and *Santa's North Pole Cookbook* – and over a half million in sales ago. Now an evergreen of holiday season shopping, the books have been translated for readers as far away as Japan, Germany, Korea and Israel. The first in the series, published in 2004, made the *New York Times* bestseller list and the books have now been collected into a handsome 735-page omnibus edition titled *The Christmas Chronicles*.

"Santa's autobiography," Guinn says, "was written during one of the hottest Texas summers on record. I'd go into my writing room, close the curtains, turn up the air conditioning and put on a CD of Christmas carols. Read any page of the book and you can rest assured that in the background Bing Crosby was singing 'White Christmas' or Gene Autry was doing 'Rudolph The Red-Nosed Reindeer.' The neighbors were getting sick of it."

Now those in his quiet neighborhood who once wanted to send him packing proudly have their own signed copies, finally aware that celebrated holiday-themed books aren't always written in-season.

Charles Dickens, who gave us the immortal Ebenezer Scrooge and Bob Cratchit, and Chris Van Allsburg, who wrote of a magical train ride to the North Pole, could have told them that.

The book-buying public, particularly parents and grandparents who have read the charming and well-researched story of how Santa became such a worldwide personality to their children, are simply pleased it was written. Over the years, youngsters have done book reports on Guinn's work, welcomed him into their classrooms, and regularly write in hopes that, since he knows the Big Guy so well, he might see that their Christmas list gets special attention.

A self-described Air Force brat as a youngster, the travels of the Guinn family provided valuable research for the books he would one day write. "I never knew if we were going to celebrate Christmas in Frankfort, Germany, Naples, Italy, or San Angelo, Texas," he recalls. "Because of that I learned a great deal about holiday traditions around the world."

The realization that he has written something that has captured a special place in the hearts of readers, Guinn admits, has been an unexpected and rewarding experience. It is a goal to which all authors, regardless of the subject matter they chose, strive.

"Jeff's Christmas books will be around for a long, long time," promises his Tarcher/Penguin editor Sara Carder. "From the moment I read *The Autobiography of Santa Claus* I felt it was destined to become a classic." Its author, she says, is now her five-year-old's favorite writer.

Burned-out vacuum cleaner aside, Guinn was clearly right to believe.

* * *

(Success continues for the 65-year-old Guinn. His book on the insane crimes of Charles Manson and his followers was a finalist for the Edgar Allan Poe Award, he's been elected to the Texas Literary Hall of Fame, and he was recently honored by the Press Club of Dallas as a Living Legend of North Texas Journalism.)

Happier Trails

= = = = = = = =

DECEMBER 2010

It was one of those starry High Desert nights and all visitors
to the Roy Rogers-Dale Evans Museum were long gone, the last
hand shaken and autograph signed. And there on the outskirts of
Victorville, California, I was being given a tour of the fort-shaped
facility which housed mementoes from one of the most remarkable
Hollywood careers in history. My host was Roy Rogers himself,
the legendary matinee idol of my youth, King of the Cowboys, the
bigger-than-life silver screen hero who rode a golden palomino
named Trigger, never lost his white hat in a fight with the bad guys
and saved the day every Saturday afternoon down at the Bijou.

I admit it. When 12-going-on 13, I dreamed of growing up to
be Roy Rogers. When he personally addressed us from the movie
or TV screen, he called us Little Buckaroos and I was proud to be
among that number.

Then, in the early stages of a book-writing career, my fantasy
came as close to reality as one could hope. It was in the late '70s
when I was asked if I would be interested in working with Roy

and his wife/co-star Dale on their autobiography, *Happy Trails*. As their literary Boswell I would help them tell their remarkable fame and faith life story.

So it was that as Roy and I were getting acquainted, walking among the displays of the museum, I got my first glimpse of the magnitude of the career I was to help chronicle. A self-professed pack rat, Roy had spent a lifetime collecting the items on display. Late into the evening we wandered among the historical artifacts of his life – posters from over 100 western movies and television shows, merchandise items – cap pistols, belt buckles, children's lunch boxes, etc. – that once filled no fewer than 12 pages of the annual Sears catalog, comic books, coloring books, and dozens of movie magazines and cereal boxes featuring his smiling likeness. We listened to recordings of his radio show that aired for nine years and heard the gentle western melodies of Roy and the Sons of the Pioneers harmonizing on "Blue Shadows on the Trail." The museum's centerpiece, of course, was a taxidermist's handiwork of the late Trigger, posed for posterity as if ready to once more carry Roy off to fight against cattle rustlers, bank robbers and various other Old West evil-doers.

For years I had not thought of those long ago California visits to Roy, Dale and their museum. Then, recently, I read that the memorabilia it once housed was to be sold off at auction by the famed Christie's in New York. Following the star couple's deaths a decade ago, attendance at the Victorville site had fallen dramatically with the entertainment icons no longer on hand to meet and greet fans. Briefly it was relocated to Branson, Missouri, but in time it became apparent that those who so idolized the couple had grown too few in number. The Saturday Matinee crowd had begun to disappear.

Too bad. I must admit to feeling a tinge of sadness when I learned that Trigger, purchased for $266,000, would be shipped off to some cable TV network official in Nebraska. Or that others of the over 1,000 items offered for sale would be scattered to the wind, owned by strangers.

Still, for me, there are memories that go far beyond price tags.

Back in their heyday, Roy and Dale (who grew up in the tiny Central Texas community of Italy) taught their young fans that good forever triumphed over evil and that every hard day's work ended with a song. A bit simplistic, you might say, but youngsters of my time bought into the notion lock, stock and barrel.

In person, Roy showed me other things. While, quite honestly, I'd have preferred that he teach me to ride, rope or fast-draw, he was an avid bowler and took it upon himself to become my coach. And, as a bonus, he once even helped me out of marital hot water.

At one time he had owned the Victorville Lanes where he and fellow league members gathered regularly. He later sold the establishment with one unusual proviso. Roy retained ownership of one lane, his to use at any time of his choosing. When he learned that I was, at best, a raw novice, he suggested we could kill two birds with one stone by conducting our interviews while he taught me the finer points of his favorite sport.

Then, there was the morning when I reported for our interview session in a mood he immediately recognized as less than upbeat. I explained that I felt sure I was deep in the dog house back home, being absent on my then wife's birthday.

"Get her on the phone," Roy urged.

I dialed the number and handed him the receiver. When the lady of the house answered, he burst into song. *"Happy birthday to you..."* Once again, the legendary Singing Cowboy had come to the rescue, saving the day.

They don't sell moments like that, even at a Christie's auction.

A Debt of Gratitude
========
MARCH 2010

Some years ago, before having learned the hard lessons of public speaking, I was invited to address a convention of librarians to whom I told a harmless joke or two, praised the gallant work they performed, and fondly recalled my book-hungry visits to the libraries of my youth.

They were eating out of my hand. Until I shared my newfound delight in the fact my 12-going-on-13 son, once not interested in so much as reading the back of a cereal box, had finally discovered the pleasure of books.

I was immediately asked what he was reading and my innocent reply was that he had begun to devour the young adult novels written by an Oklahoma woman named S.E. Hinton. Suddenly the question evolved into a full frontal interrogation. Peering at me over her glasses, my host suggested that if I had *any idea* of the subject matter of Hinton's novels I'd best perform my parental duty by returning home as quickly as possible and tossing them in the trash. A ceremonial burning might be even better.

Explaining that I had, in fact, read the parables of good and evil attached to life in a teenage gang, I admitted that they weren't exactly my cup of tea. On the other hand, they were well-written, ultimately claimed high moral ground, had won numerous awards, sold like hula hoops and, most important, were interesting enough to lure my son away from cartoon television.

I'd have been okay had I stopped there. Instead, I suggested that if hers was the attitude of all literary gatekeepers, our next generation might well be on its way to absolute, dumbfounding illiteracy.

Things sorta went downhill from there. Trust me when I say you should never argue with the folks serving the rubber chicken.

Now, come forward with me to modern day. That kid who started his reading journey with Hinton characters like Tex and Ponyboy is now 42 and a constant reader of both quality fiction and enlightening non-fiction.

And when his nine-year-old son isn't doing homework or at soccer practice, he's lost in the magical Hogwarts School adventures of bespectacled Harry Potter. His 12-year-old cousin, meanwhile, can quote entire passages from Stephanie Meyer's blockbuster *Twilight* series.

Yet when ol' granddad brags, he still gets grief: *They're wasting their time on fantasy, magic and chaste romance-vampire tales. And don't even get me started on the scary pre-teen Goosebumps stuff authored by R.L. Stine.*

See where I'm going with this?

It is my firm and unfaltering belief that the valuable habit of reading doesn't begin with the Great Works. Remember back when you couldn't get enough of Nancy Drew or the Hardy Boys; when the name Tom Sawyer was more familiar than that of Tom Wolfe? What I'm saying is we've all got to start somewhere.

And, trust me, things are just beginning to get interesting. I'm already putting together a reading list that is going to knock the kids' socks off this summer. There's *Holes*, a National Book Award winner for juvenile fiction, by Louis Sachar, and its charming sequel *Small Steps*. They're going to love the *Percy Jackson and the Olympians* series by mystery writer Rick Riordan, and a slew of sports-related novels for kids authored by famed *New York Daily News* columnist Mike Lupica.

If these don't suit, they're welcome to make their own choices.

Duncan McDougall, executive director of the Vermont-based Children's Literary Foundation, agrees that any and all reading is a good idea. "Parents concerned that their child is reading a book that is not of 'high quality' should remember that as long as children are reading they are expanding their language skills, vocabulary, and imagination. Honing their reading skills increases the chances they will succeed in school and become better prepared to read the next book, and the next."

His 12-year-old foundation, which focuses on the needs of low-income, at-risk and rural readers throughout New Hampshire and Vermont, can break your heart with the statistics it has compiled. Like the fact that over 60 per cent of low income families have not a single book at home for their children to read.

Perhaps somebody needs to better explain that if you can't

afford a Barnes & Noble gift card you might want to run down and check on a free-for-nothing deal at the public library.

That said, I hereby offer heartfelt thanks to J.K. Rowling, pleased as can be that she and her imaginary pal Harry Potter have earned so much money they're now listed in the Guinness Book of World Records. My hat's off to Stephanie Meyer for storming the bestseller lists and luring millions of young readers to her *Twilight* series. Way to go, R.L. Stine; keep cranking them out. And, bless you Susan Eloise Hinton. I shall continue to defend you wherever rubber chicken is served.

One and all, you are pointing youngsters in the right direction.

Eternal Rest

$=$ $=$ $=$ $=$ $=$ $=$ $=$ $=$

MARCH 2012

It is located a few miles south of Dallas, just beyond a quiet neighborhood and a new church, near a highway where auto repair shops and commercial storage units have multiplied in recent years. Generally overlooked by those hurrying along U.S. 67, it has been there, I'm told, since the 1940s, and, like many cemeteries of its age, has become a bit worn at the heels. I had passed it with little notice more times than I can recall.

Finally, though, curiosity called out and, on a brightly-lit afternoon, with a gentle breeze whispering through the elms and pecan trees that shade many of the gravesites, I made my way past the entrance to Cedar Hill, Texas' Pet Memorial Park to wander among the moving farewell messages of fellow pet-lovers. *"May the kitty cat angels watch over you...," "...the best friend I ever had"* ... *"If tears could bring a stairway and memories a lane, I'd walk right up to Heaven and bring you home again..."*

Trust me when I say this is no spooky, haunted place like that described by author Stephen King in his classic horror novel *Pet*

Sematary. I sensed nothing morbid or unsettling. If I had thought the place a bit strange before entering, my mind changed quickly. It was, like any cemetery, simply a memorial ground to lost loved ones, a place where bygone companionships are peacefully celebrated.

One, I suppose, has to be an animal-lover to fully understand how some feel about their dogs and cats. You saw that Associated Press holiday report, didn't you, where 68 percent of America's pets received Christmas gifts from their owners? And how about those plush pet hotels that are sprouting up nationwide?

Still, it is fair to wonder who takes a Sunday drive out to place flowers on the gravesite of an eternally resting pet. Who invests in plot fees, caskets and elaborate headstones to honor the memory of Chipper or Skippy, Lucky or Friskie? Who grieves so mightily at the loss of a non-human family member that they have it interred in such a place?

A lot of people, apparently. And such has been the case in the U.S. since 1896 when New York veterinarian Dr. Samuel Johnson had the idea of transforming his five-acre apple orchard in nearby Hartsdale into the nation's first burial ground for pets. Today the Hartsdale Pet Cemetery, just a 30-minute drive north from midtown Manhattan, is the final resting place of over 75,000 pets.

Then you've got the Sea Breeze Pet Cemetery in Huntington Beach, California, the Boston Hills Pet Memorial Park in Hudson, Ohio, the Whispering Pines Pet Cemetery in Michigan's Ypilanti Township, just to name a few.

Today, according to Donna Bethune, executive director of the International Association of Pet Cemeteries and Crematories, there are 250 such resting places registered with her organization. Add non-members and she estimates there as many as 700 worldwide. There's even an Interfaith Association of Animal Chaplains on call to conduct funeral services.

"There is a special bond between many people and their pets," says Bethune. "And there are a number of factors involved in a decision to have a pet buried in a cemetery – religious beliefs, availability of a burial site, etc. But generally it has to do with a lasting appreciation for the unconditional love and comfort the pet has given. People want a place to go and remember that."

This is nothing new, you understand. As far back as 350 B.C., when Alexander the Great's dog died, he personally led a funeral procession to the gravesite and had a stone monument erected in honor of his beloved Peritas.

It isn't even unusual, Bethune says, when inquiries come from pet owners wishing to be buried alongside their pets. "By law," she explains, "a pet can't be buried in a traditional cemetery. But, since pet cemeteries don't fall under the same regulations, it is allowed." She says her family's Oak Rest Pet Gardens in Atlanta regularly gets calls with such requests.

Which is to say the relationship between humans and their animals is clearly a powerful thing.

As I look across the room at old pals Lucy and Bud, who now spend more and more time sleeping as they get on in years, the better I understand.

World's Smallest Skyscraper

= = = = = = = =

JULY 2008

Be honest: we Texans are given to unbridled bragging. It's in the genes and heritage. From football success to vast fortunes, best, brightest and biggest, we're given to loudly boast with neither shame nor a hint of apology.

But in Wichita Falls they've turned the state's bragging art form on its head. Can you tell me another place where townspeople proudly boast of having the smallest tourist attraction to be found?

Dallas and Houston may have sparkling skyscrapers so tall that they require penthouse oxygen, but has *Ripley's Believe It or Not* ever paid them attention? Do travelers make special detours to gaze in wonder?

Visitors to the North Texas city are routinely given directions to the edge-of-downtown corner of Seventh Street and LaSalle where, since 1919, the World's Littlest Skyscraper has stood. The four-story red brick structure, just 40 feet tall, has survived tornadoes and fire and years of neglect to stand as a monument to the greed and graft of the region's long ago Oil Boom days.

This is the story visitors are told:

When the discovery of black gold in nearby Burkburnett turned thousands of Wichita County residents into instant millionaires, mineral rights deals were being made on street corners and in the shade of quickly erected tents that served as oil company headquarters. There was a desperate need for office space in Wichita Falls and a Philadelphia oil man/promoter named J.D. McMahon came running to the rescue.

With blueprints in hand, he set about quickly selling $200,000 in stock to investors caught up in the quick-buck frenzy of the day. What would result, McMahon promised, was a multi-story office building that would go up just across the street from the thriving St. James Hotel.

What, legend has it, the promoter failed to mention was that the scale of his blueprints was in inches rather than feet. Apparently too busy to keep an eye on construction, investors ultimately found themselves owners of a building that looked more like an elevator shaft than high-rise office space. The dimensions of the completed building were a closet-sized 16 feet by 10 feet. Stairwells that led to the upstairs floors occupied 25 percent of the interior.

And by the time construction was completed, McMahon was nowhere to be found. Duped investors unsuccessfully chased after the elusive scam artist and sought legal remedy only to be told they had no case. McMahon had built exactly according to the blueprints they'd signed off on.

Still, with office space in such demand, oil companies squeezed desks into the tiny space and called it home until the Boom finally fell silent. Then came the Depression and the little building was boarded up and forgotten except by flocks of pigeons that made it their roosting place. In 1931 the interior was destroyed by fire.

In 1986 the city deeded the building to the Wichita County Heritage Society which attempted to preserve it and its tall tale story. In time, however, it was again orphaned and there was steadily growing talk of having it demolished before the architectural firm of Bundy, Young, Sims & Potter was hired by the city to stabilize the downtrodden structure. So fascinated did Dick Bundy and his partners become with the historic site that in 2000 they arranged a partnership with Marvin Groves Electric, purchased the building, and launched an ambitious effort to fully restore it. New floors and stairways were put in; soon there was new electrical wiring, heating and air conditioning and a sprinkler system in case another fire ever broke out. The remodeling cost: $165,000.

"Frankly," says Dick Bundy, "it wasn't a very smart investment, but so many people wanted it preserved. And it's a unique part of our local history." Plus, he says, it is a great conversation piece. On a recent visit to Harvard University for a conference on the construction of high rise office buildings, he casually mentioned his firm's involvement with the World's Littlest Skyscraper. Before the gathering ended, Bundy was asked to the podium to tell the story of the building and his history.

Today it serves as more than an attraction for a steady stream of curious tourists. Local antique dealer Glenda Tate recently leased the building which now houses her business, The Antique Wood. Upstairs, Bundy's artist wife, Merri, has converted the third floor into her studio.

Her husband, meanwhile, is off on a new quest. Part of the colorful legend he now helps to keep alive is that it was author-adventurer Robert L. Ripley who gave the building its nickname. It is said that during a cross-country train trip Ripley stopped in Wichita Falls, discovered the structure, heard its story, and quickly sketched it while his train re-fueled. He dubbed it "The Littlest Skyscraper" in his popular daily newspaper feature. To date, no copy of the landmark publication has been located. The archives of the *Ripley's Believe or Not* cartoons, Bundy learned, were destroyed in a long ago fire.

And maybe it's just as well. No need to fool with a good legend.

* * *

(Today the "skyscraper" is listed in the National Register of Historic Places by the United States Department of the Interior and continues to draw people to an area of downtown Wichita now called the Depot Square Historic District. Bundy is still searching for that elusive Ripley cartoon.)

Finding Refuge

= = = = = = = =

SEPTEMBER 2002

During those dark and troubling days that immediately followed the event of 9/11, I was among the many who fell into catatonic disbelief of the vicious anger, the blatant evil, that had been visited upon our homeland. For days, I did nothing but stare blankly at the television, watching as images of destruction and death were pounded repeatedly into the American consciousness.

As a journalist, I had walked among the jagged ruins of the bombed-out Murrah Federal Building in Oklahoma City, watched as flames engulfed Branch Davidian leader David Koresh and his followers, seen the ravages of killer tornadoes and written of man's murderous inhumanity to man.

Haunting though such memories are, they paled in comparison to the vision of thousands dying as New York's landmark Twin Towers crumbled into an ominous boiling cloud of dust and debris.

In time, the frustration and depression that overwhelmed me

became frightening. So much so that I began a desperate search for some avenue that would lead me and mine back to a degree of innocent comfort. Somehow, somewhere, I had to get as far away from the nightmarish reality as possible, if only for a short time.

Thus, on a warm, golden evening that belied my mood, I drove to the home of my 5-year-old granddaughter and suggested an adventure. An hour's drive away, in the picturesque community of Granbury, the Brazos Drive-In, one of the few outdoor movie venues still in operation in the state, was showing a G-rated picture. It was time, I explained to her mother, for young McLean to experience the unique pleasure I had known as a child growing up in rural Texas. I stopped short of admission that I was in cowardly retreat, to a simpler time and place, free of hate and destruction and worry for the future. Instead, I talked only of watching a movie under the stars, of hot popcorn and icy sodas in the concession stand, of kids running free in the playground at the base of the screen.

McLean, carefree and oblivious to the recent tragedy that had visited the world she was growing into, quickly set about getting ready to go.

In all honesty, I cannot tell you the plot of the movie that showed that evening. Instead, I focused on a child's delight as she drank in the new and wondrous sights and sounds, giggling at something funny on the screen, meeting other children brought by parents who were no doubt there for the same reason I had come. Her joy gently pushed my own black mood aside. For the first time in days, I felt new hope and faith and optimism – calling out to me from the voice of a child.

That night, as we made our way home, my granddaughter sleeping peacefully beside me, I knew that too soon there would come a time when she and those of her generation would be called on to confront the evils and ills of an imperfect world. And I like to think they will find their own kind of strength and refuge that allows them to not only deal with it, but to move ahead in a never-ending effort to make things better.

Just as my own generation – despite time of great sorrow and setbacks, despair and doubt – has always done.

Rite of Passage

= = = = = = = =

JULY 2014

There are few less aware of the swift passage of time than the young to whom it is not yet of any real concern. Those of us a bit longer in the tooth, however, are different. We elders watch our children grow to adulthood, relieved that they've made the journey safely, finally exhaling a long overdue sigh of relief. But it lasts for only a brief time. Soon the grandchildren arrive and the process is renewed.

And, after all their youthful advances – learning to swim, ride a bike, losing a first baby tooth, hunting Easter eggs, and marching off to kindergarten toting a backpack as large as they are – they are suddenly no longer children but headed at warp speed toward adulthood. It is a fascinating process to watch. And occasionally cause for a touch of melancholy.

The other evening my granddaughter appeared in my office, a broad smile on her face as she returned the keys to my car. She had driven it, even successfully parallel parked it, and had passed her driver's test. I offered a congratulatory hug, forced a cheerful look, and watched as she happily danced away. Another of life's milestones had been achieved and the child I'd known over years that have passed far too quickly, seemed to have suddenly disappeared.

And for the remainder of the evening I considered McLean's 17-year journey. Our journey. The old cliché – *Where has the time gone?* – played in my thoughts. When had the infant I'd held just hours after her birth grown into such a beautiful young woman?

This was the same little girl I'd been picking up after school since her elementary days, the happy child who brought her friends to swim on hot summer days and built snowmen when the seasons turned cold. What became of the days of playing in the backyard sandbox and endless games of dress-up? Believing in fairies and chasing fireflies?

Over the years her grandmother and I had dutifully attended talent shows, band concerts, science fairs, awards programs, birthday parties and welcomed annual invitations to visit her parents' home on Christmas mornings to see what surprises Santa had left. We watched her cheerfully play her part in a production of *Godspell*, dazzle as Mayzie La Bird in *Seussical, Jr.*, and were in the audience as she sang with her children's chorus.

And all the while ol' Papa somehow managed to pay little attention to the fact that she was growing older. It never crossed my mind that she would eventually be talking excitedly of favorite rock bands I'd never heard of or, Heaven forbid, a Saturday night date with a new boyfriend. Or that there was no way I could help with homework that had become a foreign language to me. Suddenly she was talking of having her own car and going off to college.

On one hand I am excited by the anticipation of what her future holds. On the other, I'm saddened that a joyful past is now fast ending. Young women, I fear, have far less need for grandfathers once their attention has been directed to the exciting challenges of adulthood.

So, as she swiftly winds through her final teenage years toward a life no longer encumbered by curfews, house rules or even the need to ask ol' Papa for a ride home from school or to meet with friends, I remain ever grateful for the past – the warm memories she helped fashion with no awareness of the gift she was giving. Grandfathers and granddaughters, it is said, enjoy a unique bond. And for that I shall be forever thankful.

As I pondered the past, I recalled a long ago afternoon when she emerged from middle school. Usually cheerful and smiling, she was in tears. She and her best friend had had one of those spats common to youthful relationships and she was heartbroken. "She was my best friend," my distraught grandchild sobbed. And, while I knew the moment would pass and hurt feelings would soon mend, I could think of nothing better than a hug and promise of a stop at the local ice cream parlor to mask her pain.

Whether it would have helped or not, it should have occurred to me to assure her I would gladly be her best friend. Belatedly, I now make the offer.

What Oldtimers Do

= = = = = = = =

FEBUARY 2014

It is one of those restaurants hidden away in a shopping center on the northern edge of Dallas, a dimly-lit gathering place with celebrity photos clustered along its walls, a friendly bartender named Jennifer who has twice qualified to compete in the World Championship Chili Cook-Off, and a long history of warm, welcoming hospitality. Few of its customers are strangers. Think Cheers with a Fried Catfish Special to die for.

And every month or so a corner table of the Midway Point serves as world headquarters for a loosely-knit organization that calls itself the Oldtimers' Club. It has no officers, no dues or bylaws, is without any agenda, no minutes are kept, and anyone who actively seeks membership is automatically turned away. Over the past couple of decades its ranks have fluctuated from a half dozen to eight or ten, depending on such variables as tee times, doctor appointments, pressing honey-do requests and the occasional funeral.

It is what men on the south side of their wonder years do.

Waitress LuAnn, alerted to the meeting time, has coffee brewing and nachos warming as they begin arriving. She will dutifully take lunch orders despite having long since memorized the selection of each member and is always anxious to learn who the group has planned as its Mystery Guest. Often invited is an additional diner who will hopefully bring a fresh point of view to the gathering's discussion of major problems, most having to do with the Dallas Cowboys' troubled defense, the Texas Rangers' pitching rotation or some ill-advised youth sports coach who doesn't seem to appreciate a certain grandchild's rare athletic gift.

Among the guest experts who have joined the gathering over the years are NFL Hall of Famers Roger Staubach, Troy Aikman, Tony Dorsett and Randy White, PGA icon Don January, ex-coaches, authors and even an FBI Special Agent.

And, while everything said at the Midway Point stays at the Midway Point, trust me when I tell you that strong opinions are not in short supply. The Oldtimers have dutifully charted the Cowboys' course back to Super Bowl glory, though, clearly, the advice has gone unheeded. They instinctively know which college coaches should be hired or fired, can judge talent better than any scout on any team's payroll, and critique a local talk show host's opinion with scalpel-like sharpness.

The only verboten subject is politics, no doubt one of the main reasons for the group's longevity and the fact no meeting has ever been marred by violence or an invitation from the owner to take our discussions down the street to Jack in the Box.

Still, it is a self-proclaimed gallery of unapologetic experts. Has been since it was co-founded back in the mid-'80s by legendary Dallas Cowboys general manager Tex Schramm and Bert Rose, who had among his claims to fame the fact that he selected the nickname of the Minnesota Vikings while directing that organization in its formative days.

Over the years, alas, treasured voices have excused themselves to start up a heavenly chapter. Famed sportscaster Pat Summerall, like Shramm and Rose, is now gone. Same with gifted journalist and author Frank Luksa.

Yet the legacy of the Oldtimers continues. Over the years the empty seats have been filled. There's always a new generation that is no longer required to keep office hours. Today we've got a retired NFL standout who played in no less than five Super Bowls, award-winning writers and broadcasters, even an ex-newspaperman who is generally regarded as the ultimate expert on the assassination of President Kennedy. I'll not mention their names for fear of being excommunicated. Publicity, the group has never sought.

Now, a few are still a bit young to legitimately wear the mantel of the organization. But one day soon they'll get there. I can remember once being the youngest member. Today, just an eye-blink removed from that first informal gathering, I'm now the elder statesman. It comes with the territory.

Admittedly, an increasing number of our observations are begun with "Back in the day..." and don't dare try to convince us that younger and newer ways are somehow better.

It's just what old men do.

* * *

(In the spring of 2016, the Midway Point announced it was moving to a new location just down the street. The Old Timers dutifully followed. Old pal Blackie Sherrod, one of history's greatest and most honored sportswriters, finally excused himself in 2016 at age 96.)

No Beans in the Chili

= = = = = = = = =

JUNE 2013

A weather-beaten old cowboy poet once described the arid, wind-blasted region as the place "where the rainbows wait for rain." Another life-long resident insists his hauntingly isolated Trans Pecos corner of Texas isn't exactly the end of the world. "But" he admits, "you can see it from here."

Yet every year, thousands arrive to brave sun, sand and stark landscape for a gathering that is part tent revival, part pots-and-pans celebration. Near the ghost town of Terlingua, once a thriving cinnabar (quicksilver) mining center back in the late 1800s, they have been conducting the annual World Chili Cook-Off Championship since 1967. There, in the shadows of the Chisos Mountains, not far from deserted mine shafts and crumbling adobe walls, they gather to sing, dance, carry on, tell tall tales and, finally, see who will concoct the absolute best bowl of red.

For those like Dallas' Jennifer Hansen, the trek beats an all-expenses-paid visit to the Riviera.

Last year she was one of the 389 elite cooks who qualified for the competition. It wasn't easy. To become eligible to vie for the coveted prize, one has to earn a certain number of points in regional cook-offs throughout the year. Thus she traveled the state on weekends with her portable stove and a tongue-teasing collection of secret ingredients, cooking her way to a spot in the grand finale.

Though she ultimately returned home to her bartending job with no trophy from her rookie try, she recalls the experience fondly. "It was unbelievably exciting and I learned so much. My goal now is to qualify to go back and try again." To that end she's tweaking her recipe as we speak.

Dana Plocheck, a second-generation chili cook, understands such determination. "I started going out to Terlingua with my parents, who were competitors, when I was just a kid and first competed when I was a senior in high school," the Missouri City, Texas, resident says. By the time she and her Lady Bug Chili were announced as the 2006 winner, she had spent a decade chasing the elusive prize. "It was one of the greatest experiences of my life," she says.

They are affectionately called Chili Heads and are not in the least off-put by it. And they annually gather on the first Saturday each November from hither and yon: Texas, California and Louisiana, Wisconsin, Virginia, Mississippi and North Carolina. Last year, a delegation from Singapore joined the competition. Other hopefuls have come from England, Canada and the Virgin Islands. Attending crowds annually range from 10,000-12,000.

It began back in 1967 when famed humorist H. Allen Smith wrote an article for *Holiday* magazine in which he boldly claimed to be the world's foremost chili cook and authority. He even shared his recipe with his readers. Dallas newspaperman Frank Tolbert and pal Wick Fowler quickly shot back to say that the fact Smith's recipe included, Heaven forbid, kidney beans automatically disqualified him as a chili purist. A pot and ladle duel was challenged. Thus was born an event that even *Sports Illustrated* sent a reporter to cover. Today, it has grown to heaping serving size.

This, folks, is serious business. The sponsoring Chili Appreciation Society International (CASI) has 10,000 members and has purchased its own 320 acres where the event is now held. Over the past decade it has annually distributed an average of $1.5 million to college scholarships and charities from earnings at the Terlingua event and over 500 qualifying cook-offs it sanctions.

Richard Knight, an expatriate Texan now living in Lebanon, Tennessee, serves as CASI's executive director and has long been a competitive cook himself, finishing in the Top 10 at Terlingua four times. "Every year is like a giant family reunion," he says. "It's not unusual to find yourself cooking between a guy who spent his last 25 cents to get there and another who flew in on his private jet."

In the chili cooking world, understand, all are happily equal. Until the judges announce their decision.

Friendships aside, those who compete guard their recipes like precious jewels. Hansen, still dreaming big and eager for another try, isn't about to disclose the mixture of meat and sauce and spices that go into her brew but will say that she would never include a single kidney bean in her recipe.

"That," she explains, "is what real chili cooks refer to as a foreign object."

* * *

(Jennifer Hansen continues to win prizes and recently qualified for a spot in the 2016 Terlingua competition.)

Stuntman for the Stars

= = = = = = = =

NOVEMBER 2013

In younger days, now faded to memory, we had our innocent
dreams of growing up to be like those we admired. Some hoped to
sing like Elvis, become All-American football heroes, or maybe fly
off into the distant skies along with the pioneering astronauts of
our time. Me, I wanted to become a fast-drawing, straight-shooting
western movie star or maybe an Olympic champion. Sparing you
the O. Henry ending, be aware that I fell light years short on both
counts.

Dean Smith, a fellow traveler through my boyhood '50s, fared
much better.

It's not likely that you New Generation readers will remember
him, but those of us with slightly higher mileage and reasonably
good recall do. A University of Texas track standout, Dean came
home from the 1952 Olympic Games in Helsinki with a gold
medal earned as a member of the U.S. 400-meter relay team. Then,

after flirting briefly with professional football as a member of the Los Angeles Rams, he became a familiar face to movie and TV watchers for decades.

Things came naturally to the young man who was both the state sprint champion and a gifted rodeo performer during his schoolboy days back in little Graham, Texas.

It was at the Palace Theater on Saturday afternoons, watching B-westerns that seemed always to have titles like *Gunfight at Black Rock*, when his own dream began to take shape. "I was a big fan of the westerns as a kid," he recalls, "and knew that someday that's what I wanted to do."

And, with the help of a friend-of-a-friend named James Bumgarner (you know him best by his screen name, James Garner), he got his Big Break. Garner made some calls, Dean got an audition, and soon was riding and roping, chasing down runaway stagecoaches and engaging in more mock fistfights than you could shake a stick at. Lord only knows how many times he was shot and killed on screen. He quickly became one of Hollywood's most-wanted stuntmen, stepping in for the big name stars when time came for the dangerous dirty work.

If you were watching closely, you saw him working alongside John Wayne in a half dozen of the Duke's movies. And that was him doubling for a Who's Who of Hollywood, like Roy Rogers, Robert Redford, Dale Robertson, Michael Douglas, Ben Johnson, Bruce Dern and Frankie Avalon. It was Dean – red wig, skirt and all – who stepped in to take a second story fall for Maureen O'Hara in *McLintock!* He was among the defenders in *The Alamo*, portrayed Kit Carson in *Seven Alone*, and saved the day in *Stagecoach*. And that's just for starters.

While his first love was the westerns, their popularity ultimately faded, forcing him to seek other roles that required his special talents. The TV reporter in Steve Spielberg's first feature film, *Sugarland Express?* That was Smith. He was a member of the ship's crew in *P.T. 109* and even had his moments in Stephen King's *Christine.* Had the makers of *The Lonely Guy* (in which Smith doubled Steve Martin) not made the poor choice to cut the scene, you would have watched him dangling from a helicopter high above the New York skyline.

"But, I was never a daredevil," he says. During his career, he was injured only once, suffering a broken rib while doubling Redford in *Jeremiah Johnson.* He missed but one day's work on the film.

And he continued to run. When an Orange Bowl crowd was needed for a scene in *Black Sunday,* a match race was organized between the 44-year-old Olympian and fleet Miami Dolphins receiver Nate Moore, 20 years his junior. Smith won.

Today he's 81, back home in Texas, living with wife Debbie and teenage son Finis on his 1,000-acre ranch on the Clear Fork of the Brazos. There he watches over his herd of longhorns and still rides his palomino, Yella Fella, when not off being recognized for past achievements. He's been inducted into the Stuntmen's Hall of Fame and the Texas Sports Hall of Fame. The list of accolades bestowed on him fills a complete page in his recently released autobiography, *Cowboy Stuntman,* authored with fellow Texan Mike Cox.

"When I first got into the movie business," he says, "it was my hope to one day be a big cowboy star like Roy Rogers or Gene Autry or John Wayne. But, it just wasn't to be. My job was to be a stuntman, and it was a wonderful way to earn a living."

Which is to say Dean Smith came a lot closer to his childhood dream than most of us.

* * *

(Now 84, Dean Smith was recently elected to the Texas Track and Field Hall of Fame.)

Pinball Passion

= = = = = = = =

SEPTEMBER 2014

We were the best of friends back in that long ago summer, spending sun-bleached days dutifully tending our two-man lawn-mowing enterprise. Then, on warm and carefree evenings we wiled away our time at baseball games, playing miniature golf, and endlessly driving past the swimming pool and circling the parking lot of the Dairy Delight. If you saw *American Graffiti*, you got the picture of our late '50s lifestyle.

What made it all possible was the fact that Stan, a year older and a grade ahead, had a car.

It was, as I recall, an almost idyllic time – unless our travels took us past an edge-of-town truck stop cafe. Inside was my nightmare. Lined up side-by-side against one wall were a half dozen brightly-lit pinball machines, lights flashing and bells ringing as players' scores soared. Once there, I was as doomed as a helpless Stephen King character.

Stan was a full-fledged, unapologetic addict to the flipper and steel ball games. Once he started playing, he couldn't stop until all his lawn-mowing money had been shoved into the machines, one dime at a time. No fan of the one-man sport, I was trapped. My only escape was to place a call to some other friend and ask for a ride home. I can't tell you the number of nights I left Stan standing over the glass-topped "Neptune" or "Humpty Dumpty" game (all pinball machines, you understand, have catchy names), determined to beat his previous high score and, if really fortunate, earn a free game.

My dedicated friend, it turns out, was a man ahead of his time.

Little did I know that the day would come when there would be a Pinball Hall of Fame and Museum in Las Vegas, collectors' clubs worldwide, and more competitive tournaments and festivals than you can shake a stick at. The International Flipper Pinball Association currently lists and ranks 22,700 tournament-playing members.

And all this time you've assumed high tech toys like Xbox and PlayStation had caused the death of that leisure activity which had its origin during the reign of Louis XIV.

Pinball machines, once located in restaurants, bars, laundromats, grocery stores, movie theater lobbies, and arcades, are still alive and well. Not so much in their original public haunts now, but in the game rooms of homes from hither to yon.

There was a time when the games were viewed as a social curse that encouraged gambling. It was in 1976 when expert player Roger Sharpe went before the New York City Council in an effort to do away with its ban of the machines. Demonstrating a predicted shot with a high degree of difficulty, he successfully made his case that pinball was a game of skill, not chance.

"Pinball," Sharpe said, "is just simply fun, a fantasy world under glass."

Paul McKinney, a product management consultant, has 20 of the games in his Cedar Hill, Texas, rec room, the oldest a 1932 model; the most cherished, one called "Joker Poker," which he remembers riding his bike to a neighborhood convenience store to play when he was 13.

"Pinball machines," he says, "are true pieces of Americana and, in my view, remarkable works of art."

When he's not attending estate sales and swap meets or checking the Internet and classified pages in search of one of the only 200 "Mystery Castle" games produced – "It's my pinball Holy Grail!" – he is one of the organizers of the annual Texas Pinball Festival. During its 12-year history it has become the largest such event in the country.

"The interest in pinball brings people from all walks of life together," says collector Ed VanderVeen, owner of over a dozen games. When he and wife Kim aren't searching for another to add to their formal dining area-turned-game room, Ed serves as a police sergeant.

On a recent weekend in the Dallas suburb of Frisco, almost 3,000 visited to walk among the 400 games on display. Men and women, young and old, from throughout the United States and as far away as Australia and England, were swept up in nostalgic wonder at the sights and sounds of row after row of games with names like "Night Rider," "Strike Zone" and "Star Gazer."

My old pal Stan would have felt he'd arrived in Pinball Heaven.

Golden Memories

= = = = = = = =

MARCH 2014

It goes without saying that we attach special meaning to those baubles that serve as reminders of our touchstone achievements. It might be the trophy on the mantel that proves that you finished first in the Left-Handed Mixed Singles Bowling League back in the day or the plaque proving that you were once applauded as the Regional Widget Salesman of the Year. For the more gifted who have shown brightly on loftier stages, there's the Nobel Prize, the Motion Picture Academy's Oscar, the Heisman Trophy, Super Bowl ring or Olympic gold medal.

Cherished reminders all, they are proudly displayed, polished to a fine sheen... and occasionally lost. It is the stories of the latter misadventures that have fascinated me during a lifetime of interviewing those who have stood on award stands and delivered acceptance speeches.

For instance, when the legendary Jesse Owens returned from

Berlin's 1936 Olympics with four gold medals, he said he reluctantly agreed to loan them to a traveling carnival for nationwide display. Alas, they soon went missing. The Olympic bigwigs were alerted to the tragedy and struck a duplicate set for Owens. Then, his house burned down and those were destroyed. Finally, a third set was struck and presented Owens. One of his medals, which he later gave friend and entertainer Bill (Bojangles) Robinson, made headlines recently when it sold at auction for $1.47 million to California collector Ron Burkle, who also happens to be the owner of William Faulkner's Nobel Prize for Literature medal.

And don't get me started on Hattie McDaniel's story. The first African American to receive an Academy Award following her 1940 role as a slave servant in *Gone with the Wind*, her Best Supporting Actress award was displayed in the Howard University drama department until it mysteriously disappeared in the early '70s. Years of detective work have not succeeded in locating it.

I can't tell you how many tales I've heard about championship rings dropped in lakes, lost on golf courses or, in at least one instance, gambled away in a poker game. According to his autobiography, heavyweight champ Muhammad Ali angrily tossed his Olympic gold medal into the Ohio River after being refused service in a Lexington, Kentucky, restaurant following his triumphant return home.

Thus my reason for traveling to little Dublin, Texas (pop. 3,800), a couple of hours drive southwest of Dallas, to visit the four-year-old Ben Hogan Museum. I wanted a look at the Hickok Belt awarded the town blacksmith's son when he was voted the nation's premier professional athlete in 1953.

Well, actually, it isn't the original handed out by the Rochester, New York, belt-making Hickok Manufacturing Company to the legendary winner of 64 tournament titles, including the Masters, the PGA, U.S. and British Opens. That one was stolen from Fort Worth's Colonial Country Club trophy room in the late '70s. By the time the culprit was apprehended, the solid gold award, valued at over $10,000 when it was originally presented, had been melted down and the four-carat diamond, ruby and sapphire as well as the 26 diamond chips imbedded in it were being offered to the highest bidder.

Undaunted, officials of the Ben Hogan Foundation and Colonial, with historian Ben Matheson on point, went in search of the mold for the award, determined to have it replicated.

In time a second generation Hickok went to the United States Golf Association Museum in Bernards Township, New Jersey, there to be displayed in its just-completed Ben Hogan Room. And in 2012 it, too, was stolen by some thief, likely unaware that it was now only gold-plated and the jewels synthetic. The trophy was never retrieved.

Back to the mold they went. The latest incarnation, looking exactly like the original, right down to the alligator skin belt it is attached to, is now the proud centerpiece of the Dublin museum which is located right around the corner from the site of the old Hogan Blacksmith Shop.

When Matheson and Robert Stennett, executive director of the Hogan Foundation, arrived last November to deliver it, they spent considerable time wandering among the fascinating and tastefully displayed memorabilia collected in what was once the office of a Dublin doctor. "Mister Hogan," Matheson told museum director Karen Wright, "would be so proud of this place."

Which is to say it's well worth the trip. And, Wright points out, the building's security system is state of the art. Thieves be warned.

Love of Language

= = = = = = = =

SEPTEMBER 2013

With a dime's worth of luck, Bryan Garner won't be reading this. That way he won't discover any participles dangling or double negatives popping up or pesky adjectives and adverbs misplaced. Heaven forbid that there's a punctuation goof or a word misspelled. As one of the world's pre-eminent English language experts, he can spot things like that a mile away.

This is a guy, believe it or not, who, as a child, would sit in his room *reading* the dictionary while his buddies were expanding their literary horizons with the comic book derring-do of Superman and Batman. More than one teacher back in his Canyon, Texas, school days lost an argument over proper usage of a word to the young and precocious Bryan. Once, on a family skiing vacation, he discovered a book titled *Usage and Abusage: A Guide to Good English* and became so engrossed in it that he never made it onto the slopes.

As a toddler, his booster seat at the family dining table was a hefty edition of *Webster's Second New International Dictionary* which was provided by his grandfather, a Texas Supreme Court justice for 20 years.

Even before he passed the bar exam after law school at the University of Texas, Garner was publishing papers in the same academic journals that included those written by his professors. His first book, a dictionary of legal terms that Oxford University Press would publish, was done by the time he was a 24-year-old law clerk.

Now, 30 years later, the number of books he's written has grown to 20, including two which he co-authored with Supreme Court Justice Antonin Scalia (their *Making Your Case: The Art of Persuading Judges* received the 2009 Burton Award as the Law Book of the Year), and his resume reads like that of a linguistic Renaissance man. In addition to writing, he serves as editor-in-chief of *Black's Law Dictionary* (the Bible of the legal profession), annually conducts a couple of hundred seminars in the U.S., England, Australia and Hong Kong for lawyers wanting to make their briefs and writs less legal gobbledygook, and is today recognized as the nation's premier lexicographer. Which is a "writer of dictionaries." You can look it up.

He serves as a Distinguished Research Professor of Law at Southern Methodist University and is an avid book collector. Among the 35,000 volumes in his library are over 4,000 dictionaries in languages that range from Chinese to Swahili. The oldest, written in Latin, was published in 1491.

Additionally, a visitor can browse shelf after shelf of works on Shakespeare, Winston Churchill, lexicography pioneer Sam

Johnson, countless sets of law books and 1,000 volumes, dating back as far as 1700, on English grammar.

"Books," he says, "are so intellectually substantial. There are certain kinds of scholarship that you can't find on the Internet. You have to have books."

It is a philosophy that has evolved from a lifelong fascination with words. From his early days it trumped any aspiration to stand in front of a jury and litigate cases. What he opted to do, instead, was open his Dallas-based LawProse Inc., in 1990 and begin offering fellow lawyers a better way to communicate. To date, he estimates he's lectured to 95,000 attorneys at his seminars. And his books on legal writing have become must-have tools of the trade. Writing in her Foreword to *Garner on Language and Writing*, Supreme Court Justice Ruth Bader Ginsburg notes that the author's books are constantly at arm's reach on her writing desk and are assigned reading for all of her law clerks.

"Word for word," Garner says, "lawyers are the highest paid writers in the world. But the literary tradition in the profession is probably the worst. As with any other form of prose, legal writing should be accessible to the masses."

To see that come to pass has been his life's goal.

His lofty credentials, of course, occasionally cause social problems. "Sometimes," he admits, "people are a bit guarded, as if I'm going to be judgmental of how they use the language. One of the most common things I hear from someone who has learned what I do is, 'I'm really going to have to watch what I say.'"

Such caution, he says, is unnecessary. "I make mistakes myself."

With all due respect, that's a bit hard to believe.

Bumper Sticker Blues

= = = = = = = =

MAY 2014

Before reading further please be advised that the following lecture on social behavior has not been inspired by road rage, any recent fender bender, or increase in automobile insurance rates. Despite what some in my family might say, know that I'm a gentle traveler who takes note of speed limits, acknowledges crossing guards, and brakes for all manner of furry creatures in my path.

I've dutifully heeded the warning against texting and using my cell phone while driving (mainly because electronic gadgets remain a mystery to me). I buckle up so as not to face stiff fines and make sure the kiddies are safely strapped into their car seats. Obeying these commands, however, does nothing to eliminate the major concern I have when traveling highways and byways.

When, I want to know, is someone going to do something about bumper stickers – those inane and irritating little vinyl notices that cover today's vehicles like wet leaves?

If I see one more warning that "If You Can Read This You

Are Following Too Close," I may start taking the bus. If the guy behind the wheel doesn't want me to read it, why is it plastered across his rusty, dented bumper in the first place?

They provide far too much information. On even a short trip down to the grocery store I can learn what sports teams a driver supports, his or her political leaning, the church the family attends, parks and tourist attractions they've visited, where they go for ice cream and pizza, the organizations in which the car owner holds membership, and that they dutifully recycle. While one proudly announces that "My Kid is an Honor Student at Such-and-Such Middle School," there's another in the next lane boasting that "My Kid Can Whip Your Honor Student." We've got bumper sticker conversations, for Pete's sake.

There are even people who collect them like bubble gum cards.

Says Mike Karimi, manager of Irving, Texas-based LookingGlass Graphic and Sign which has been producing bumper stickers for 27 years, "The people who order them are ones who have a message they wish to send, be it political, promotional or personal." The trick, he says, is to state one's case with a minimum number of words.

They'll give you two-bit advice ("If everything's coming your way, you're in the wrong lane"), sarcasm ("Don't laugh, its paid for and ahead of you"), tortured wit ("You can't be late until you show up"), put downs ("Idiots surround me") and shameless boasts ("I Ate the 72-ounce T-bone at Billy Jack's Feed Barn"). Just follow the minivan ahead and you can profile those inside better than the FBI. In addition to everything mentioned above, you'll learn that they have a "Baby On Board" and, Heaven forbid, the breed of dog waiting for them to get home and fill the food dish ("I (Heart) My Doberman"). And does that slow-moving truck driver really want me to respond to "How's My Driving?"?

Who comes up with this stuff? Apparently the sources are widespread and growing. Individuals, clubs, schools, candidates for office, and businesses large and small purchase them from neighborhood print shops for the sake of advertising. If you're shopping for something humorous, stop in at any truck stop, gag gift store or go online. You write it, someone out there will print it. Karimi's company has filled orders ranging from as few as 250 to 10,000. They are, he suggests, the auto-owner's answer to t-shirt slogans and body tattoos. Some customers, he notes, not only plaster then on their cars but their boats as well. Clearly, this thing is spreading.

Truth is, I'm a bit tardy with my complaint. This is hardly a new problem. Historians who seem to care about such matters, point out that the first known bumper stickers were attached to Henry Ford's Model A's. (Thank goodness the forerunning Model T's didn't come equipped with bumpers.) Advertisers, we're told, first jumped on the bandwagon in the '40s when a tourist attraction called Rock City in Lookout Mountain, Tennessee, started putting promotional stickers on every visiting car in the parking lot. Look what they started.

I'm thinking of having Karimi print me one that reads "Ban Bumper Stickers." Not all that catchy, I admit, but you've got to start somewhere. On the other hand, perhaps I should simply heed the suggestion of one I saw recently on a Stone Age vintage VW bus that read "Stop Reading My Bumper Stickers."

How I wish I could.

Taking the Torch

= = = = = = = =

DECEMBER 2013

From office windows high above the playing fields the two men can look upon a constant reminder of the legacy that has been handed down to them. It is there at the home stadium of their NFL Kansas City Chiefs, and in the Dallas suburb of Frisco where their Major League Soccer team, FC Dallas, plays.

Eternally greeting fans with arms folded and his trademark smile is a bronze statue of one of professional sports' greatest innovators. There, to forever be remembered, is Lamar Hunt, the man thousands of admirers still lovingly refer to as "Uncle Lamar." He was, like them, a sports fan first and foremost. His nickname as a child, in fact, was "Games." Family members still tell the story of the time the Hunt dog gave birth to a large litter of puppies, half which were white, half black. The young Lamar quickly divided them into two teams and ingeniously devised a competition for them.

It was that lifetime love that prompted him to pioneer the American Football League that battled the NFL before ultimately being welcomed into the established fold. By 1969 his Chiefs had become Super Bowl champions. The name for the showcase event was credited to Hunt who got the idea while watching his children play with a simple little toy called a Super Ball.

He also brought European soccer into the American consciousness. Professional tennis flourished thanks to his visionary World Championship Tennis organization. Among the founders of the NBA Chicago Bulls was Hunt, who quietly retained an 11 percent share of the team that was passed on to his family following his death in 2006. For his energetic efforts, Lamar Hunt was inducted into the Pro Football Hall of Fame, the National Soccer Hall of Fame and the International Tennis Hall of Fame.

And it was all accomplished with a quiet, behind-the-scenes dignity that belied the wealth and fame of the son of legendary oil magnate H.L. Hunt. Before Chiefs home games, he always visited the parking lots, talking with fans. His home number could be found in the phone book. Lamar was never one to flaunt his successes.

Still, as the story goes, a journalist, who noted that he was losing a staggering $1 million annually in the early days of his pro football venture, approached Lamar's billionaire dad for his thoughts on the crisis. "A million a year, huh?" the elderly Hunt responded. "At that rate, he'll go broke in a hundred or so years."

Today, according to *Forbes*, the Chiefs franchise is worth almost $1 billion.

Now come his sons, stepping into large shoes. Today, Clark,

48, serves as chairman and CEO of the NFL Chiefs while Dan, 36, watches over all things related to the Hunt Sports Group's Major League Soccer endeavors. Youngsters who once enjoyed trout fishing trips with their dad and were delighted that he was on hand to watch their pee-wee soccer games, they now continue to employ his quiet strategies as their own.

The apples haven't fallen far from the tree. They have inherited their dad's energy, resolve and easy nature.

Both see their primary responsibility to be good stewards and to continue to advance their father's dreams. "He was a great mentor, a visionary and an innovator whose first concern was always the fans," recalls Dan. "That's now our role."

Brother Clark agrees. As he now oversees the operation of the Chiefs, he is daily reminded of the magnitude of the task his dad embraced. "It was one thing to stand next to my father and see the spotlight shining on him. Being in a public role is a completely different challenge," he says.

Clark's goal is to bring more championships to Kansas City. Dan, meanwhile, has visions of the day when soccer stadiums throughout the U.S. are filled to capacity and American teams are recognized as equals to the established foreign clubs.

In truth, they say, there was never a specific time when their father announced that they would eventually be given the reigns of the family business. Lamar Hunt was more subtle, simply inviting them to join him at league gatherings and including them in business meetings.

Dad would be pleased to know they've learned their lessons well.

Magic at Mary's Café

= = = = = = = =

NOVEMBER 2014

Be forewarned that I am neither a restaurant critic nor a card-carrying foodie. Words like haute cuisine and gourmet dining are not part of my vocabulary. That said, I will take anyone on and give points when it comes to the subject of chicken fried steak. Trust me, I've done my homework hither and yon throughout the southwest.

And in the rural Texas hamlet of Strawn (pop. 650), a 90-minute drive west of Dallas, is the Mother Church of the popular comfort food. At Mary's Café, where from 11 a.m. to 11 p.m. daily (except for Thanksgiving and Christmas), true artists are at work in the kitchen of a low-ceiling building that, back in the 1920s, served as the town's lone service station.

People come from destinations near and far, pouring inside to get a table and soak up the roadhouse décor – neon beer signs and framed, autographed photos of celebrities who have dropped in.

On any given day, the gravel parking lot may be filled by

traveling biker clubs, church groups, a limo filled with birthday or anniversary celebrants, busloads of young athletes in search of a post-game meal or hunters en route to the region's deer leases. And, of course, pickup trucks driven by the locals.

"I'd say 98 percent of my customers are from out of town," owner Mary Tretter says. They come regularly from the Dallas-Fort Worth area, from New Mexico and Colorado, even as far away as Atlanta, Georgia. A family stopped in recently, explaining they'd heard about the place when they encountered a fellow traveler in China who was wearing a Mary's Café t-shirt and singing the praises of the restaurant's fare.

When Mary celebrated her café's 25th anniversary by offering free chicken fried steak to Sunday customers, the turnout was three times the population of the little community. Goodness only knows how many might have been on hand had not a rattling hailstorm interrupted the day. To demonstrate the popularity of her chicken fried steak, she turns to arithmetic: Last year, she says, she purchased 46,880 pounds of cutlets that were pounded, floured and cooked into the celebrated dish.

All of which is testimony to the entrepreneurial genius of the sassy, fun-loving, too-young-looking-to-be-57 Tretter who freely admits that when she bought the place back in 1986 she couldn't even cook a palatable bowl of cream gravy. When she became owner of a struggling little 89-seat restaurant called The Polka Dot and placed her own name over the door, customers were few. At the time her resume included dish washing and waiting tables, something she started doing at age 14. ("I didn't even go on my Senior Trip when I graduated high school," she says. "I was working.")

Self-taught, she is today proprietor of one of the best known out-of-the-way eating stops in Texas. With several expansions over the years, including an outdoor patio, customer capacity has grown to 300 and, while her menu offers everything from T-bone steaks to seafood, burgers to Mexican dishes, it is her restaurant's signature chicken fried steak that is the magnet.

Its preparation is begun only after an order is turned in. No warming lamps or pre-cooking allowed. Yet, only the most adventuresome selects the large portion from the menu. It literally hangs over the plate. Add the bowl of pepper gravy, a mound of French fries, toast and a salad, and there's food enough to keep a small army on the move.

Which is to say they serve no ordinary chicken fried steak at Mary's Café. It is cooked on a flat-iron griddle rather than heavily battered and deep-fried. So protective of her recipe is Mary that employees are required to sign a non-disclosure agreement carefully worded by an attorney.

And be aware that she's a hands-on owner, working alongside her 30-member staff. Three days a week, she waitresses. Today a modestly proclaimed "decent cook," she's in the kitchen on Friday, Saturday and Sunday. Wednesdays she takes off to be with her grandkids.

"Our goal is simple," she says. "Fill the plate with good food, make it look nice, and keep the customers happy. If they leave here hungry, it's their fault."

As she rose to begin her work day, I scanned the menu – and, as always, ordered the chicken fried steak.

Before
Six Flags
= = = = = = = = =
AUGUST 2005

It was a time before summer fun meant Six Flags, SeaWorld,
Wet 'n Wild, multiplex matinees or shopping mall game rooms.
In the carefree summers of my childhood, the magical wish of
West Texas youngsters was to make a trip to the Eastland County
community of Cisco. Three miles north of town, beneath what
historians assured us was the world's largest hollow dam, was Lake
Cisco Recreation Park – Cisco Pool, for short.

As a 13-going-on-14-year-old, I was awed. It was said to be the
world's largest concrete swimming pool – 700 feet long, 300 feet
wide, and filled with 14 million gallons of cool, crystal-clear water. I
clumsily demonstrated my timid version of derring-do on the diving
boards and towers, swings and slides, secretly hoping to impress the
pretty sunbathers lounging on the small, grass-carpeted island that
separated the shallow and deeps ends. Doo-wop and rock and roll
blared from the adjacent two-story wooden building that housed
dressing rooms, a concession stand and an upstairs roller rink.

After swimming, there was miniature golf on a challenging course, minus the hokey windmill and clown-faced hazards of latter day layouts. For smaller tykes, there were amusement rides. A stone gazebo was the centerpiece of the tree-shaded picnic area, and a zoo with native wildlife ranging from a panther to javelinas was tucked into the nearby bluffs.

In adventurous moments, out of my parents' protective sight, I climbed the steep steps of the entryway to the dam's spooky interior and walked along a concrete concourse from one end to the other. In the privacy of the dark, damp tunnel, more than one first teenage kiss was exchanged. Or so I'm told.

At night, young and old danced under the stars to the music of legends like Bob Wills and his Texas Playboys.

Families who wished to make a weekend of it could rent one of the small stone-walled cabins at the base of a nearby hillside. A 25-cent permit was all that my father needed to fish for perch, crappie and bluegill on the backside of the dam. On Fourth of July weekends, visitors could attend the annual Independence Day Beauty Pageant sponsored by the park owners.

Cisco Pool was the go-to destination for family reunions, company picnics or school trips. On summer Saturdays, cars would be backed up along Highway 183, waiting to pay a $1 per head fee to enter the rural playground.

The park was built in 1929, flourished well into the '60s, and finally closed in 1975. By the time Cisco's city fathers and the state Health Department agreed that the pool was in need of a prohibitively expensive facelift, the glory days were already gone. So were the zoo, the amusement rides, the celebrity entertainers

– and the crowds. The guest cabins were boarded up. In time, fire destroyed the building that housed the roller rink.

On a recent trip, I found only its skeletal remains. The pool now holds a few feet of murky water that feeds the flourishing weeds and bushes. Snakes sun themselves along the cracked concrete walls. Finding the miniature golf course required wading through waist-high weeds, and the iron bars that once housed the zoo animals are tangled and rusted, protecting nothing. The inside of the dam is scarred with ugly graffiti.

Cisco Pool's ghostly legends are all that have survived. Some people still insist that a construction worker helping build the massive damn fell to his death, his body never retrieved but simply buried beneath the tons of cement being poured. And there are those who say that for years they could hear the plaintive cries of a black panther that escaped the zoo and wandered along the chalky cliffs.

I take such tales with a grain of salt. Still, when one visits the old park and stands quietly, gently nudging the imagination, he can hear the laughter of children, gleefully splashing, and the music wafting through the mesquites. And, in doing so, he can once more feel the soothing warmth of summers long past.

Lasting Impact

= = = = = = = =

FEBRUARY 2009

Another West Texas summer day had reached into wilting double-digits, and Tom Rodman was standing at the 12th floor window of downtown Odessa's tallest building, silently gazing out at the parched landscape. "Out there," he finally said, pointing toward a distant spot where the untrained eye sees nothing but ragged mesquite, wind-whipped dust devils, and the rhythmic movement of mechanical hobbyhorses pumping oil from deep beneath the Permian Basin.

Seven miles beyond the city limits, past the rows of Mexican food restaurants, truck stops, and drill-equipment businesses, is a geographical wonder that has fascinated the aging oil and gas attorney since boyhood.

"Out there" is the Odessa Meteor Crater, the second-largest impact site in the United States, taking a backseat only to the famed and visually stunning Barringer Meteor Crater, near Winslow, Arizona. In brag-crazy Texas, where second-best of anything generally draws little more than a dismissive scoff, Rodman stubbornly stands as self-appointed promoter and caretaker of what he insists is a scientifically important locale and a must-see tourist attraction.

Family aside, the jagged, rock-strewn old crater is the love of Rodman's life. It is because of his tireless efforts that the site is now recognized by the National Park Service as a national landmark and that a state-of-the-art museum now sits near the crater.

The energetic Rodman delights in recalling how things might have been 60,000 years ago, when a 300-pound piece of iron-rich stone flamed through the Earth's atmosphere at 27,000 miles per hour and collided with a force that scientists estimate surpassed the energy created by the atomic bomb dropped during World War II.

"When I was a boy," he says, "my father owned the ranch land that bordered the area where the crater is located. I spent a lot of time playing there, always saw it as a magical place. Back then, a large tree had grown in the base (of the crater), and I'd sit in its shade and try to imagine what this part of the world might have looked like back when the meteor hit." And, with that, he's describing how this arid landscape was once verdant swampland instead of blowing sand and brush. In his mind's eye, he can see the prehistoric mammoths and three-toed horses that once roamed the region now populated by jackrabbits, rattlesnakes and pickups.

It was not until 1929 that geologists determined the scarred hole in the Ector County countryside was, indeed, a spot where 100,000 cubic pounds of limestone has been displaced by a meteor's impact. The site, estimated to have previously been 100 feet deep, has changed with the passage of time. Although the crater's rim is still distinctive, thousands of years of sand and silt have left the crater itself no deeper than many of the man-made gravel pits that pockmark the region.

Local legend has it that a rancher discovered the crater in 1892. Later, another resident found a fist-size metallic rock in the area of the crater in 1920 and, thinking it an interesting oddity, gave it to his banker. It sat on the banker's desk for several years until a visiting geologist saw it and suggested sending it to museum authorities for analysis. It was ultimately determined that the stone contained particles of iron, nickel, cobalt and copper – all components of a meteorite. In time, geologists and mining engineers would explore the area, convinced that a giant stone from the stars was buried beneath the layers of silt.

By the early 1940s, a shaft had been dug 165 feet deep into the heart of the crater, and long trenches were jack-hammered across the depression. Workers did unearth the fossilized remains of a mammoth and found hundreds of pounds of meteorite fragments. Scientists, however, finally determined that the meteorite had shattered into millions of small pieces on its low-angle impact.

Today, visitors to the museum can view many of those fragments, collected from as far as two miles away, and also stroll along a path that winds through the crater.

And more likely than not, they'll bump into Rodman, still the dreamer, still fascinated by the history of his childhood playground.

"Dad's enthusiasm for the crater has never diminished," says Rodman's lawyer son, Jimmy. "When my brothers and I were kids, he would take us out there and tell us the stories of what happened long, long ago. His dedication to its preservation is amazing."

Texas state representative George West, who successfully lobbied for the $500,000 appropriation that made the Odessa Meteor Crater Museum a reality, agrees with Jimmy Rodman. "I first visited the crater when I was a 12-year-old Cub Scout," he recalls. "It has been

Tom Rodman's dream, his vision, to call attention to this remarkable landmark

"It just took the rest of us a while to catch up with him."

* * *

(Interest in the meteor crater and its museum continues, with over 10,000 visitors annually. Now 85, Tom Rodman regularly drops by.)

About the Author

= = = = = = = =

Carlton Stowers is the author of more than 40 books, two of which have won the Mystery Writers of America's Edgar Allan Poe Award. His journalism, which has appeared in numerous national and regional publications, has been cited by the North American Travel Journalists Association, the State Bar of Texas, and the Dallas and Houston Press Clubs.

He won the A.C. Greene Award given to a distinguished Texas author in 2007 and is a member of the Texas Literary Hall of Fame and the Texas Institute of Letters.

A native Texan, he lives in Cedar Hill.

CPSIA information can be obtained
at www.ICGtesting.com
Printed in the USA
FFHW021313261118
49656064-54019FF